PERU TRAVEL GUIDE

2025:

Explore the Heart of the Andes: Culture, Adventure, and Hidden Gems Await.

BY

LOUIS S. HARPER

DISCLAIMER

This travel guide is provided for informational purposes only. The information contained herein is believed to be accurate and reliable as of the publication date, but may be subject to change. We are not making any warranty, express or implied, with respect to the content of this guide.

Users of this guide are responsible for verifying information independently and consulting appropriate authorities and resources prior to travel. We are not liable for any loss or damage caused by the reliance on information contained in this guide.

Information regarding travel advisories, visas, health, safety, and other important considerations can change rapidly. Users are advised to check for the most up-to-date information from official government and travel industry sources before embarking on any trip.

Travel inherently involves risk, and users are responsible for making their own informed decisions and accepting any associated risks.

TABLE OF CONTENT

MAP OF PERU

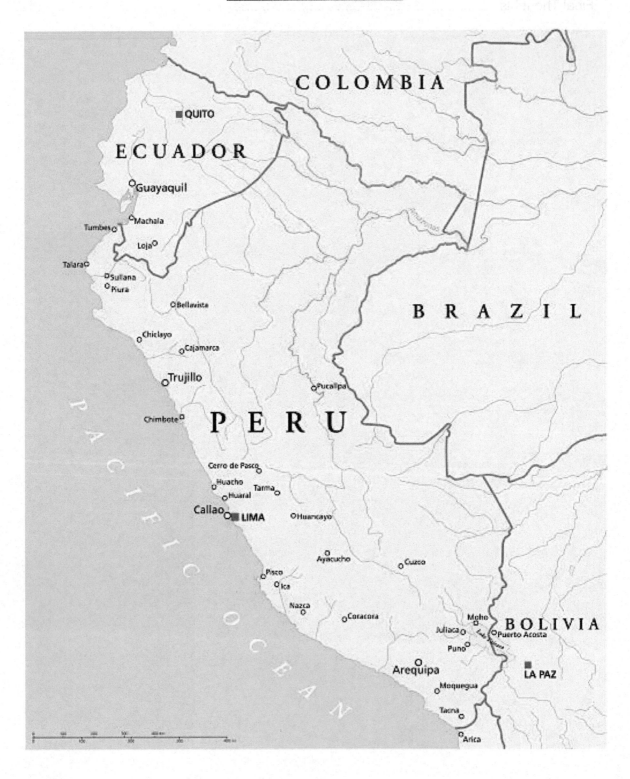

Introduction

1.1 Welcome to Peru

Peru is a land of wonders, where ancient history meets breathtaking natural beauty. Nestled in South America, it's a country that boasts some of the world's most iconic landmarks and diverse ecosystems. Whether it's your first visit or one of many, Peru has a way of captivating the hearts of its visitors. Imagine standing amidst the awe-inspiring ruins of Machu Picchu, walking along the vibrant streets of Cusco, or hearing the rhythmic melodies of traditional Andean music echoing through the mountains.

This guide is designed to be your companion as you embark on a journey filled with adventure, cultural discovery, and unforgettable memories. Peru is more than a destination; it's an experience that stays with you forever. From the bustling capital city of Lima to the serene waters of Lake Titicaca, Peru invites you to uncover its rich tapestry of history, cuisine, and natural splendor. Get ready to be amazed at every turn.

1.2 Why Visit Peru?

Peru is a treasure trove of attractions and experiences, offering something unique for every type of traveler. Here's why you should make Peru your next destination:

- **Rich History and Culture**: Peru is home to the remnants of the mighty Inca Empire, including the legendary Machu Picchu, a UNESCO World Heritage Site. Beyond the Incas, the country's history is shaped by a blend of indigenous traditions, colonial influences, and modern innovations. Museums, archaeological sites, and cultural festivals provide a glimpse into Peru's vibrant past and present.
- **World-Class Cuisine**: Lima, the capital, is often referred to as the "Gastronomic Capital of the Americas." Peruvian cuisine has gained global recognition for its bold flavors and innovative dishes. Don't miss staples like ceviche, anticuchos, and the fusion flavors of Nikkei (Japanese-Peruvian) cuisine.
- **Natural Wonders**: From the peaks of the Andes to the depths of the Amazon rainforest, Peru's landscapes are nothing short of spectacular. The Colca Canyon, one of the world's deepest canyons, offers breathtaking views, while the Amazon River basin teems with exotic wildlife. For sand dunes and beaches, head to the coastal areas like Huacachina or Mancora.
- **Adventure**: For thrill-seekers, Peru offers hiking, trekking, and adventure sports. The Inca Trail, one of the most famous treks in the world, leads you through stunning landscapes to the gates of Machu Picchu. There's also sandboarding in the desert, paragliding in the Sacred Valley, and white-water rafting in the Amazon.
- **Unique Festivals**: Peru's vibrant festivals, such as Inti Raymi (Festival of the Sun) and the Puno Week celebrations, showcase the country's deep cultural roots. These events are a colorful blend of music, dance, and ancient rituals.

1.3 What to Expect from This Guide

This comprehensive guide is your key to unlocking the best of Peru. It's structured to help you plan every aspect of your trip, whether you're dreaming of exploring ancient ruins, savoring local dishes, or immersing yourself in Peru's natural wonders. Here's what you'll find:

- **Detailed Destination Guides**: Explore iconic sites like Machu Picchu, Cusco, and the Sacred Valley. We'll also introduce you to hidden gems like the Chachapoyas region and the pristine beaches of the north.
- **Travel Tips**: Learn practical advice on transportation, currency, safety, and navigating cultural norms. We'll cover essentials like how to handle high-altitude travel and what to pack for each region.
- **Food and Drink Recommendations**: Discover Peru's culinary delights, from street food to fine dining. We'll highlight must-try dishes, the best restaurants, and tips for navigating local markets.
- **Outdoor Adventures**: Find information on hiking trails, nature reserves, and adventure sports, complete with difficulty levels, costs, and insider tips.
- **Cultural Insights**: Understand the traditions, customs, and etiquette that make Peru such a fascinating destination. We'll delve into the history behind festivals, art, and local crafts.

Whether you're a first-time visitor or a seasoned traveler, this guide aims to provide the tools and inspiration you need to make your journey unforgettable.

1.4 Peru's Geography & Climate

Peru's geography is as diverse as its culture, making it a paradise for travelers who love variety. The country is divided into three distinct regions:

1. **Coast (La Costa)**: The narrow coastal strip is a land of contrasts, with vast deserts, fertile valleys, and bustling cities. Lima, Peru's capital, is located here, offering a mix of colonial architecture, modern attractions, and a stunning Pacific coastline. The climate is mild and dry, with temperatures rarely exceeding thirty degrees Celsius.
2. **Highlands (La Sierra)**: The Andes Mountains dominate this region, creating a dramatic backdrop for picturesque villages, ancient ruins, and terraced farmlands. Popular destinations like Cusco, Arequipa, and Puno are nestled

here. The highlands experience two main seasons: the dry season (May to October) with clear skies and cool nights, and the rainy season (November to April), which brings lush landscapes.

3. **Jungle (La Selva)**: The Amazon rainforest covers nearly sixty percent of Peru's landmass, making it one of the most biodiverse areas on Earth. Cities like Iquitos and Puerto Maldonado serve as gateways to this lush region, where you can explore wildlife-rich reserves and indigenous communities. The jungle is warm and humid year-round, with a pronounced rainy season.

Understanding Peru's geography and climate is essential for planning your trip. For instance, while the coast is great for beach outings in December, trekking in the Andes is best from May to September. Packing accordingly will ensure you're prepared for the varying conditions across regions.

Chapter 2: Planning Your Trip

Planning your trip to Peru is an exciting step toward discovering one of South America's most fascinating destinations. To ensure a smooth and memorable journey, it's important to prepare well in advance. This chapter will guide you through everything you need to know—from choosing the best time to visit and understanding travel logistics to staying safe and healthy while exploring this diverse country.

2.1 Best Time to Visit

The ideal time to visit Peru depends on which regions you're interested in exploring. Peru's varied geography means that different areas experience different climates, so planning accordingly will ensure you make the most of your trip.

For the Andes & Machu Picchu (Cusco, Sacred Valley, Inca Trail):
The dry season (May to October) is the most popular time to visit Peru's Andean highlands. The weather is usually sunny with cool nights, making it perfect for trekking and sightseeing. The months of July and August see the highest number of tourists, so expect larger crowds and higher prices. If you're looking to avoid the peak season, the shoulder months of April, May, or September to October are great alternatives.

For the Amazon (Iquitos, Puerto Maldonado):
The best time to explore the Amazon is during the dry season (April to November). While the jungle is humid and rainy throughout the year, the dry season offers lower water levels, allowing easier access to the jungle and better wildlife viewing opportunities. The wet season (December to March) brings more rainfall and higher water levels but is also ideal for those interested in birdwatching or witnessing the lush, green rainforest at its fullest.

For the Coast (Lima, Paracas, Arequipa):
The Peruvian coast experiences mild temperatures all year, with a distinction between the cooler, overcast months (May to October) and the warmer, sunnier period (November to April). The warm season is perfect for enjoying outdoor activities along the coast, such as surfing, beach trips, and desert excursions.

Tip:
If you'd like to avoid the crowds and benefit from lower prices, consider traveling during the shoulder season, typically between April and May or September and October.

2.2 Getting There

Getting to Peru is relatively straightforward, as the country is well-connected by air, land, and even water.

By Air:
Lima is the main international gateway to Peru, with direct flights from major cities in North America, Europe, and South America. Most flights from international hubs land at Jorge Chávez International Airport. Once you've arrived in Lima, you can easily catch domestic flights to popular tourist destinations like Cusco, Arequipa, and Iquitos. Flights from Lima to Cusco typically take just over an hour.

By Land:
Peru shares borders with Ecuador, Colombia, Brazil, Bolivia, and Chile, and it's possible to travel overland from these countries. There are bus routes from neighboring countries, but these trips can be quite lengthy, so it's best to plan your route well in advance if you choose this option.

By Sea:
Though less common, traveling by sea is an option for reaching the Amazon region, particularly via Iquitos, which is only accessible by river or air.

2.3 Health & Safety Tips

Health Considerations:

- **Altitude Sickness:** If you're traveling to high-altitude areas like Cusco or the Sacred Valley, be aware of altitude sickness. Symptoms can include headaches, dizziness, and nausea. To reduce the risk, take it easy during your first few days, drink plenty of water, and avoid alcohol and heavy meals. Some travelers also take altitude medications, but it's best to consult with a healthcare provider before using them.

- **Traveler's Diarrhea:** This is common for travelers to Peru. Avoid drinking tap water and be cautious with street food. Bottled or filtered water is safer, and always wash your hands before eating or after using the bathroom.
- **Mosquito-Borne Diseases:** Malaria and dengue fever are present in some parts of Peru, especially in the Amazon region. To protect yourself, wear long sleeves and use mosquito repellent, particularly if you're staying in rural or jungle areas.

Safety Tips:

- **Personal Safety:** Peru is generally safe for tourists, but like many places, you should be cautious of petty theft. Keep your valuables secure and be mindful of your surroundings, especially in busy areas like markets and transportation hubs.
- **Scams and Overcharging:** Some unlicensed taxi drivers or street vendors may try to overcharge tourists. Stick to reputable services and always agree on prices before accepting a ride or purchasing goods.

2.4 Vaccinations & Travel Insurance

Vaccinations:

Before traveling to Peru, it's important to make sure your routine vaccinations are up-to-date, including MMR (measles, mumps, rubella), diphtheria, tetanus, and pertussis. In addition, consider the following recommended vaccines:

- **Hepatitis A and B**
- **Typhoid**
- **Yellow Fever** (especially for travel to the Amazon or rural areas)
- **Malaria Prophylaxis** (for travel to malaria-prone areas)

Consult your doctor at least a month before your trip to make sure you have the right protection for the regions you plan to visit.

Travel Insurance:

Travel insurance is highly recommended for any trip to Peru. It should cover medical emergencies, trip cancellations, lost luggage, and travel delays. While healthcare in major cities is generally reliable, access to medical care in remote or rural areas may be limited. Make sure your policy includes emergency evacuation coverage.

2.5 Currency & Banking

Currency:
The official currency of Peru is the **Nuevo Sol (PEN)**, often abbreviated as "S/." The exchange rate typically hovers around 3.7 to 4 soles per 1 USD, but it's wise to check the current rate before traveling.

ATMs & Credit Cards:
ATMs are widely available in larger cities like Lima and Cusco, but less so in rural areas. Major international debit and credit cards (Visa, MasterCard) are accepted in most hotels, restaurants, and shops in tourist areas. However, smaller businesses or those in more remote regions may only accept cash, so it's always good to have local currency on hand.

Currency Exchange:
It's usually more convenient to exchange currency once you arrive in Peru, as rates are generally better than those offered by foreign exchange services. You can exchange money at the airport, exchange houses, or major banks. Always compare rates before exchanging a large amount of cash.

2.6 Essential Travel Apps & Websites

In today's digital world, a number of travel apps and websites can make navigating Peru easier and more enjoyable. Here are some of the most helpful tools:

- **Google Maps** – Perfect for navigating cities like Lima and Cusco, especially when exploring on foot or by public transport.
- **MAPS.ME** – A great offline mapping tool, ideal for navigating remote areas without access to Wi-Fi or data.

- **Uber & Cabify** – These ridesharing apps are available in major cities and are often safer and more convenient than traditional taxis.
- **Booking.com & Airbnb** – Convenient platforms for booking accommodations ranging from hotels to unique, locally-run guesthouses or private rentals.
- **TripAdvisor** – Offers reviews and recommendations for everything from restaurants to tours and local attractions.
- **Komoot & AllTrails** – These trekking apps are useful for planning and navigating hiking routes, particularly for those venturing onto the Inca Trail or other high-altitude treks.

Useful Websites:

- **Peru.travel** – The official tourism site, providing up-to-date information about Peru's attractions, festivals, and travel tips.
- **Sky Airline & LATAM** – Helpful for booking domestic flights to various Peruvian cities.
- **Inca Trail Reservations** – The official website for securing permits for the famous Inca Trail trek to Machu Picchu.

By thoroughly preparing for your trip, you'll ensure that your time in Peru is as enjoyable and hassle-free as possible. From selecting the right time to travel and knowing how to get there to understanding health precautions and using helpful apps, this chapter provides all the information you need to get started on your Peruvian adventure. Safe travels!

Chapter 3: Visa & Entry Requirements

Traveling to Peru is relatively straightforward for many international visitors, but it's important to understand the visa and entry requirements based on your nationality. This chapter will guide you through the visa process, offer tips for navigating immigration smoothly, and provide advice for families traveling with children.

3.1 Visa Overview for Different Nationalities

Peru has a relatively liberal visa policy, with many nationalities able to enter the country without the need for a visa. However, the requirements vary depending on your nationality and the purpose of your visit. Here's an overview of what you can expect.

Visa-Free Entry for Many Nationalities:
Citizens of many countries, including the United States, Canada, the United Kingdom, Australia, the European Union (EU) member states, and several Latin American nations, can enter Peru without a visa for tourism purposes. This visa-free entry is typically granted for stays of up to **183 days**.

Countries That Require a Visa:
Some nationals, particularly from countries outside of Latin America and Europe, may need a visa to enter Peru. This includes travelers from countries like India, China, and several African and Middle Eastern nations. If you are from a country that requires a visa, you must apply for one before traveling.

Visa on Arrival:
In rare cases, certain nationalities may be eligible for a visa on arrival. However, this is subject to approval at the immigration checkpoint and may not be available in all circumstances. It's always recommended to check with the nearest Peruvian embassy or consulate before your trip to confirm whether you need a visa.

Types of Visas:

- **Tourist Visa**: For those visiting Peru for tourism purposes. This is the most common type of visa for visitors.
- **Business Visa**: For travelers entering Peru for business meetings, conferences, or trade events.
- **Student Visa**: For those enrolled in a recognized educational institution in Peru.
- **Resident Visa**: For individuals intending to live and work in Peru for an extended period.

Tip:

If you plan to stay for an extended period or travel to multiple countries in South America, be sure to check if you need any additional paperwork or special visas for other countries.

3.2 Immigration Process & Entry Tips

Entering Peru is typically a straightforward process for tourists, but it's helpful to know what to expect at immigration. Here's what you'll need to know when you arrive.

Immigration Procedures:

Upon arrival in Peru, all travelers must proceed through immigration control, where you'll need to present:

- Your **passport**, which should be valid for at least **six months** beyond your planned departure date.
- A completed **entry form** (usually provided on the plane or available at the airport), where you'll be asked to declare the purpose of your visit (tourism, business, etc.).
- **Return or onward ticket**: Immigration officers may ask to see proof of your return or onward travel out of Peru.
- **Proof of funds**: In some cases, especially for travelers staying for an extended period, you may be asked to demonstrate that you have sufficient funds to support yourself during your stay.

Stamping and Duration of Stay:

After submitting your documentation, the immigration officer will stamp your passport with the allowed duration of stay, typically **90 days** for most tourists. However, this can vary depending on your nationality and the discretion of the immigration officer. If you are planning to stay for a longer period, you can extend your stay once in Peru (subject to approval) at the **Migraciones** office.

Tip for Immigration:

When entering Peru, make sure to carefully check the date on your entry stamp, as it may affect your departure plans. If you overstay your permitted duration, you may be fined, and in some cases, denied re-entry into Peru or other South American countries in the future.

3.3 Traveling with Children

Peru is a family-friendly destination, but there are some important considerations when traveling with children, particularly regarding immigration procedures and entry requirements.

Entry Requirements for Children:

When traveling with minors, immigration procedures may be slightly different. Children under 18 may not require a visa, but they still need to meet the following requirements:

- **Passport**: Children must have their own passport. If a child is included in a parent's passport, that passport will no longer be valid for international travel. Make sure the child's passport is valid for at least **six months** beyond the planned departure date.
- **Peru Entry Form**: Minors must also complete an entry form upon arrival.

Parental Consent:

If only one parent is traveling with a child, or if a child is traveling with someone who is not their legal parent, the Peruvian authorities may require a **parental consent letter** from the non-accompanying parent(s). This letter must be notarized and outline permission for the child to travel. The letter should include the details of the trip, such as dates, destinations, and the accompanying adult's contact information.

Traveling with an Unaccompanied Minor:
If a child is traveling alone, or with a group other than their parents, they must also have a signed **Parental Authorization**. This document should be notarized and include the specific details of the child's travel plans. In some cases, airlines and border authorities may have additional documentation requirements for unaccompanied minors.

Health Requirements for Children:
Traveling with children may require additional health precautions. Be sure to check the vaccination requirements for minors. Malaria prophylaxis or vaccinations like yellow fever may be recommended for children traveling to certain parts of Peru, such as the Amazon. Always consult with a pediatrician well before your trip to ensure your child is up-to-date on necessary vaccinations.

Tips for Traveling with Children:

- **Altitude:** Children are also susceptible to altitude sickness, so take extra care when traveling to high-altitude destinations like Cusco or the Sacred Valley. Ensure they stay hydrated, take it easy for the first few days, and avoid overexertion.
- **Pack Snacks and Entertainment:** Long bus or flight rides can be tiring for children. Be sure to bring snacks, toys, or entertainment to keep them occupied during travel.
- **Family-Friendly Accommodation:** Peru has a wide range of accommodation options that cater to families, including family rooms and accommodations with kitchenettes. Hotels in major cities or popular tourist destinations often offer special services for families traveling with children.

Tip:
If you're planning to visit Peru's more remote areas or embark on a trek like the Inca Trail, check with your tour operator in advance to confirm their policies and recommendations for children. Some trekking agencies have age restrictions, while others may offer specialized family tours.

Final Advice: Whether you're traveling solo or with family, it's crucial to familiarize yourself with the visa and entry requirements before your trip. Being well-prepared ensures a smooth arrival process and minimizes any potential delays or complications at immigration. By knowing what documents you need, understanding how to navigate entry procedures, and having the proper permissions in place for children, you'll be able to focus on enjoying your adventure in Peru without stress.

Chapter 4: Transportation

Navigating Peru's vast and diverse landscape requires knowledge of its various transportation options. Whether you're exploring the bustling cities like Lima or venturing into remote Andean towns, Peru offers a wide range of travel choices to suit all types of travelers. This chapter covers transportation within major cities, air travel within the country, bus options, trains, taxis, rideshares, and car rentals. We also offer tips for traveling in more remote regions, including the Andes.

4.1 Getting Around Lima & Major Cities

Lima, the capital, is a sprawling urban hub with plenty of transportation options. However, heavy traffic can make getting around challenging. Here's an overview of how to move around Lima and other major cities like Cusco and Arequipa.

Public Transport in Lima:

- **Metropolitano Bus System:**
  The Metropolitano is a rapid-transit bus system with dedicated lanes, allowing you to avoid traffic jams. It connects key areas like Miraflores, San Isidro, and the historic center.
    - **Cost:** A one-way ride costs about **S/ 2.50 (USD $0.65)**.
- **Lima Metro:**
  Although the metro system currently has just one line, it provides a quick and affordable way to get around, connecting central Lima with southern districts.
    - **Cost:** Fares range from **S/ 1.50 to S/ 2.50 (USD $0.40 to $0.65)**.
    - **Website:** http://www.limabus.pe/

Taxis and Ridesharing:

- **Taxis:**
  Taxis are easily found throughout Lima, but it's best to use registered taxis or apps to ensure safety. Always confirm the fare or ask the driver to use the meter.

- **Cost:** A typical fare starts at **S/ 5 to S/ 10 (USD $1.30 to $2.60)** within the city center, with longer trips costing around **S/ 20 (USD $5.20)**.
- **Uber & Cabify:**
  Both Uber and Cabify are widely used in Lima and other cities, offering safer and more predictable pricing than street taxis.

Cycling in Lima:

Lima is becoming increasingly bike-friendly, especially in neighborhoods like Miraflores. Many bike-sharing services are available for tourists.

- **Cost:** Rental rates typically range from **S/ 10 to S/ 30 per hour (USD $2.60 to $7.80)**.

4.2 Domestic Flights & Air Travel Tips

Given Peru's vast size, domestic flights are often the most efficient way to reach distant cities, particularly in the Andes or Amazon regions. Air travel is also ideal for saving time between major tourist destinations.

Airlines Operating in Peru:

- **LATAM Airlines:**
  The largest airline in Peru, LATAM offers extensive domestic routes connecting cities like Lima, Cusco, Arequipa, and Iquitos. They also provide international services.
  - **Website:** https://www.latam.com/
- **AeroCondor:**
  AeroCondor is a smaller carrier with routes to regional destinations such as Arequipa, Pucallpa, and Puerto Maldonado.
  - **Website:** http://www.aerocondor.com.pe/
- **Sky Airline:**
  Known for its budget-friendly fares, Sky Airline operates flights to various Peruvian cities like Cusco, Arequipa, and Piura.
  - **Website:** https://www.skyairline.com.pe/

Air Travel Tips:

- **Book Early:** To secure the best prices, book domestic flights at least 2-3 weeks in advance, especially during high tourist seasons (June to August).
- **Baggage Fees:** Be mindful of baggage policies. Most airlines offer a carry-on and one checked bag for free, but low-cost carriers often charge for checked luggage.
- **Security:** Expect standard security checks at Peruvian airports, but additional inspections may occur for international flights.

Cost Estimates:

- A one-way flight from Lima to Cusco typically costs **S/ 150 to S/ 300 (USD $40 to $80)** depending on the season and airline.

4.3 Bus Travel in Peru

Buses are one of the most common and affordable ways to travel across Peru, especially between major cities and tourist destinations. The bus system is well-developed, and there are several reliable companies to choose from.

Top Bus Companies:

- **Cruz del Sur:**
  This reputable bus service offers various levels of comfort, from basic to luxury, and operates routes to cities like Arequipa, Cusco, and Puno.
    - **Website:** https://www.cruzdelsur.com.pe/
- **Oltursa:**
  Known for its punctuality and comfort, Oltursa connects major destinations such as Lima, Trujillo, and Cusco.
    - **Website:** https://www.oltursa.pe/
- **Movil Bus:**
  A budget option for travelers, Movil Bus offers affordable routes to cities like Lima, Arequipa, and Tacna.
    - **Website:** https://www.movilbus.com.pe/

Bus Fare Estimates:

- A bus ride from Lima to Cusco typically costs between **S/ 60 to S/ 200 (USD $15 to $52)**, depending on the class of service (economy, semi-cama, or cama suite).

Bus Travel Tips:

- **Comfort Levels:** For long journeys (e.g., 10+ hours), consider upgrading to a more comfortable seat (e.g., semi-cama or cama suite).
- **Security:** Be vigilant with your belongings, especially on long-distance buses where there may be opportunities for pickpocketing.

4.4 Trains and Scenic Journeys

Train travel in Peru provides an opportunity to experience the country's natural beauty at a slower pace, especially to visit places like Machu Picchu.

PeruRail:
Operating trains to key destinations like Machu Picchu, PeruRail offers a range of services, including Expedition (economy), Vistadome (with panoramic windows), and the luxurious Belmond Hiram Bingham.

- **Website:** https://www.perurail.com/

Inca Rail:
Another train service that operates routes to Aguas Calientes (the closest town to Machu Picchu), Inca Rail also offers budget to premium train options for travelers.

- **Website:** https://www.incarail.com/

Train Fare Estimates:

- A round-trip train from Ollantaytambo to Machu Picchu ranges from **USD $60 to $500**, depending on the service class.
- **Belmond Hiram Bingham** offers luxury experiences at **USD $500+** for round-trip tickets.

4.5 Taxis, Rideshares & Public Transportation

Taxis:
Taxis are plentiful in cities like Lima and Cusco, but make sure to choose registered taxis or use rideshare apps for added security. Confirm the fare in advance or request that the driver uses the meter.

Rideshare Services (Uber & Cabify):
Both Uber and Cabify operate in Lima, Cusco, and Arequipa, providing more reliable and transparent pricing than traditional street taxis.

Public Buses:
In addition to the Metropolitano system, public buses are available in Lima but may be less reliable and crowded. It's best to use them for short trips during daylight hours.

4.6 Renting a Car in Peru

Renting a car in Peru can be an option for travelers wishing to explore at their own pace, especially in areas outside major cities. However, driving in the country requires caution due to local driving habits and challenging road conditions.

Car Rental Options:
International agencies like **Hertz**, **Avis**, and **Budget** operate in Lima, Cusco, and Arequipa, as well as several local companies such as **Rent Car Peru** and **Peru Rent a Car**.

- **Cost:** Rental prices start around **USD $30 to $50 per day** for a basic vehicle.

Driving Tips:

- **Road Conditions:** In cities, traffic can be intense, while rural roads may be winding or poorly maintained.
- **GPS & Navigation:** GPS is essential for navigating both cities and more remote locations.

- **Insurance:** Make sure to get comprehensive insurance to cover accidents and any damage to the car.

4.7 Navigating the Andes & Remote Areas

When heading into the remote Andes or other isolated regions, travel options become more limited. A 4x4 vehicle or guided tour is often the best option to access areas like the Sacred Valley or Colca Canyon.

Private Tours & 4x4 Vehicles:
For remote destinations, hiring a private driver or joining a group tour is highly recommended. Many tour companies offer specialized vehicles capable of handling the rough terrain.

Local Transport:
In remote areas, shared minivans or **collectivos** are often used for inter-town travel, providing an affordable way to reach destinations, though they can be crowded.

Altitude & Health Tips:
When traveling to high-altitude regions like Cusco or the Sacred Valley, take time to acclimatize. Drink plenty of water, avoid exertion, and consider medications for altitude sickness if necessary.

Chapter 5: Accommodation

Peru provides a diverse selection of accommodations for every type of traveler. From high-end luxury hotels to eco-conscious boutique stays and affordable hostels, there's a perfect place to stay no matter your budget or preferences. Whether you're in Lima, Cusco, the Sacred Valley, or a remote Amazonian lodge, you'll find accommodations that enhance your journey. In this chapter, we'll highlight the best places to stay, from premium options to unique and budget-friendly choices.

5.1 Top Hotels & Luxury Stays

Peru boasts a variety of high-end hotels, particularly in its major cities and key tourist spots. These luxury accommodations offer exceptional service, fine dining, and exclusive experiences, providing the perfect base for exploring the country's culture and natural beauty.

Hotel Belmond Miraflores Park

- **Location:** Miraflores, Lima

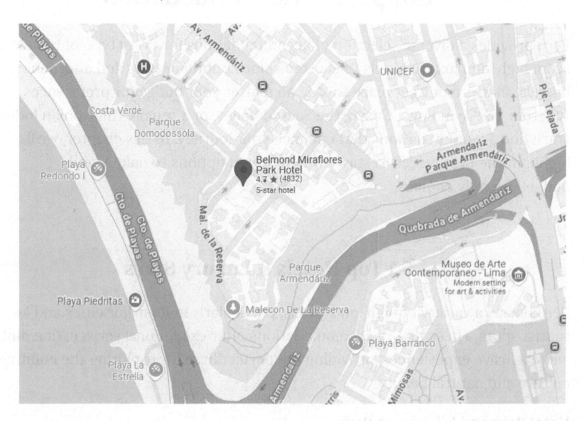

- **Overview:** This five-star hotel offers stunning ocean views, elegant rooms, a rooftop pool, fine dining, and a spa, making it a top choice for those seeking a luxurious experience in Lima.
- **Price:** From **USD $300+** per night.

Palacio Nazarenas by Belmond

- **Location:** Cusco

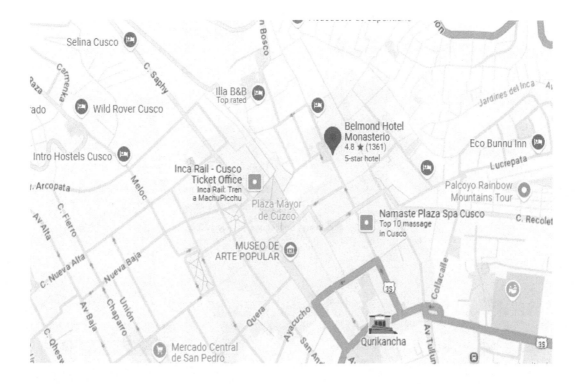

- **Overview:** Set in a restored palace, this luxury property offers exceptional services, a heated outdoor pool, and luxurious rooms. It's perfect for those wanting to experience history and luxury in Cusco.
- **Price:** From **USD $450+** per night.

Tambo del Inka, a Luxury Collection Resort & Spa

- **Location:** Sacred Valley

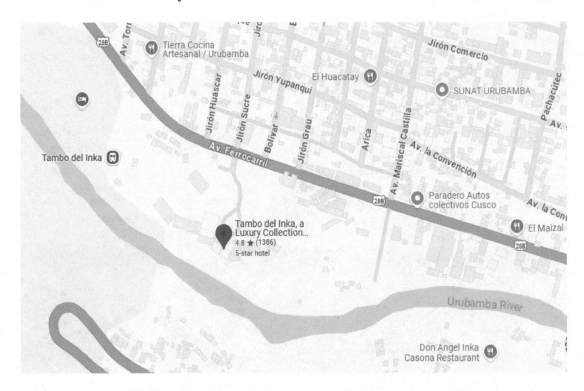

- **Overview:** Located in the Sacred Valley, Tambo del Inka offers breathtaking views of the Andes, a full-service spa, an outdoor pool, and easy access to Machu Picchu. Ideal for luxury travelers looking for tranquility and adventure.
- **Price:** From **USD $350+** per night.

5.2 Boutique & Eco-Friendly Hotels

For travelers seeking a more intimate, sustainable experience, Peru is home to a growing number of boutique hotels and eco-lodges. These accommodations often emphasize environmental responsibility while providing personalized service and immersion in local culture.

Inkaterra Machu Picchu Pueblo Hotel

- **Location:** Aguas Calientes (Machu Picchu)

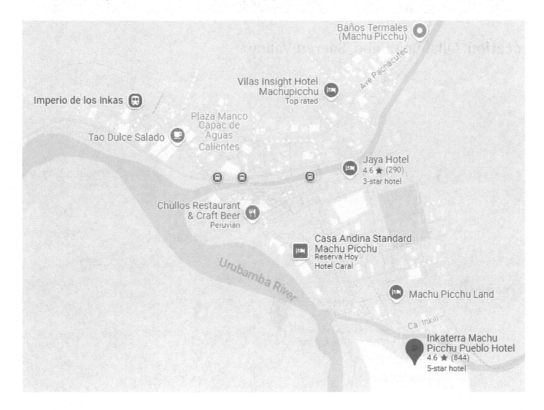

- **Overview:** Nestled in the cloud forest, this eco-luxury hotel blends into the natural environment, offering organic gardens, wildlife tours, and guided hikes. A tranquil retreat for nature lovers.
- **Price:** From **USD $250+** per night.

El Albergue Ollantaytambo

- **Location:** Ollantaytambo, Sacred Valley

- **Overview:** This sustainable hotel offers rustic charm, local cultural experiences, and farm-to-table dining. Situated near the Ollantaytambo ruins, it's a great base for exploring the Sacred Valley.
- **Price:** From **USD $100+** per night.
- **Website:** https://www.albergueolantaytambo.com/

La Casona de Yucay

- **Location:** Yucay, Sacred Valley

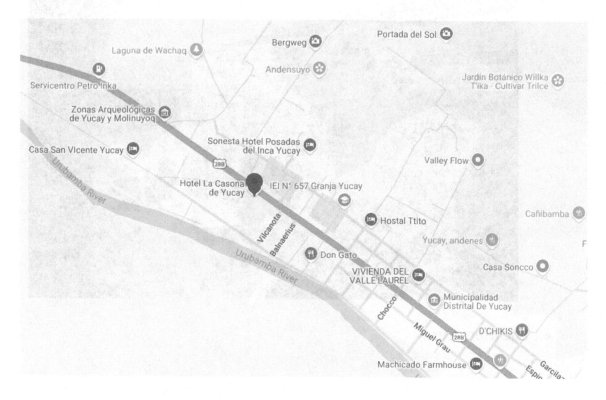

- **Overview:** This charming boutique hotel occupies a 16th-century colonial mansion, offering peaceful surroundings, organic food, and cultural experiences. Ideal for guests who want a unique and sustainable stay.
- **Price:** From **USD $120+** per night.
- **Website:** https://www.lacasonadeyucay.com/

5.3 Hostels & Budget Accommodation

For budget-conscious travelers, Peru offers an abundance of affordable hostels and guesthouses. These options provide comfortable and social accommodations, often in central locations, with the opportunity to meet fellow travelers.

Pariwana Hostel Cusco

- **Location:** Cusco

- **Overview:** A popular hostel with a lively, social atmosphere, Pariwana offers dorms and private rooms, a large courtyard, and free breakfast. It's perfect for backpackers looking to explore Cusco's historic center.
- **Price:** From **USD $15-25** per night (dorm rooms).
- **Website:** https://www.pariwanahostels.com/

Hostel Kokopelli

- **Location:** Cusco and Lima

- **Overview:** This eco-friendly hostel chain offers a welcoming vibe with modern facilities, clean rooms, and fully equipped kitchens. Kokopelli is perfect for budget travelers who want a comfortable stay.
- **Price:** From **USD $20-30** per night (dorm rooms).
- **Website:** https://www.kokopellihostels.com/

The Point Hostel

- **Location:** Lima and Mancora

- **Overview:** Known for its surf-friendly atmosphere, The Point Hostel offers a laid-back environment with beach access, a pool, and social events. It's ideal for budget travelers and those looking for a fun, relaxed vibe.
- **Price:** From **USD $12-20** per night (dorm rooms).
- **Website:** https://www.thepointhostels.com/

5.4 Unique Stays: Treehouses, Haciendas & More

For a more memorable experience, consider staying in one of Peru's unique accommodations, such as treehouses in the Amazon, historic haciendas in the Sacred Valley, or luxury eco-lodges surrounded by nature.

Treehouse Lodge

- **Location:** Amazon Rainforest, Iquitos

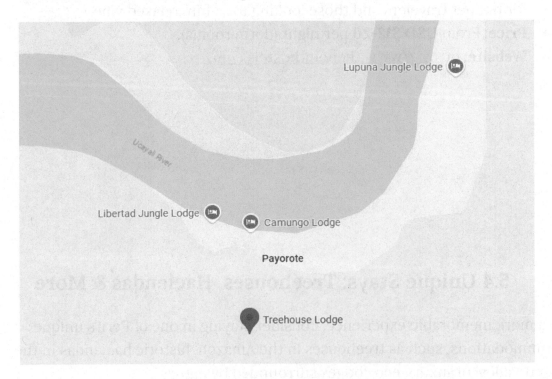

- **Overview:** A truly unique experience, Treehouse Lodge offers luxury cabins suspended among the trees, providing a deep immersion in the Amazon rainforest. Guests can enjoy guided tours, wildlife watching, and river excursions.

- **Price:** From **USD $150+** per night (all-inclusive).
- **Website:** https://www.treehouselodge.com/

Hacienda Urubamba

- **Location:** Sacred Valley

- **Overview:** A restored colonial hacienda nestled in the Sacred Valley, offering a charming escape with horseback riding, cultural workshops, and easy access to local ruins.
- **Price:** From **USD $180+** per night.
- **Website:** https://www.haciendaurubamba.com/

Inkaterra Reserva Amazonica

- **Location:** Amazon Rainforest, Puerto Maldonado

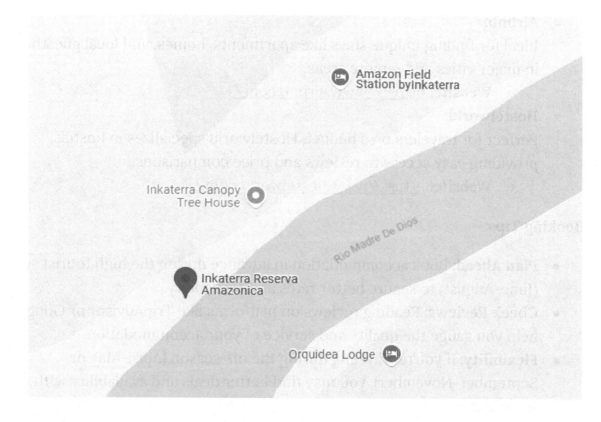

- **Overview:** Located in a secluded area of the Amazon, Inkaterra Reserva Amazonica provides a fully immersive rainforest experience, with luxury cabanas, guided jungle treks, and river cruises.
- **Price:** From **USD $300+** per night (all-inclusive).

5.5 Booking Tips and Platforms

Booking accommodation in Peru is simple, thanks to numerous online platforms and local resources. Whether you prefer booking in advance or last-minute, there are plenty of options to secure the best deals.

Popular Booking Websites:

- **Booking.com:**
  A global platform offering a variety of accommodations, from luxury hotels to budget-friendly options.
  - **Website:** https://www.booking.com/

- **Airbnb:**
  Ideal for finding unique stays like apartments, homes, and local guesthouses in major cities and remote areas.
  - **Website:** https://www.airbnb.com/
- **Hostelworld:**
  Perfect for travelers on a budget, Hostelworld specializes in hostels, providing easy access to reviews and price comparisons.
  - **Website:** https://www.hostelworld.com/

Booking Tips:

- **Plan Ahead:** Book accommodation in advance during the high tourist season (June-August) to secure better rates and availability.
- **Check Reviews:** Reading reviews on platforms like TripAdvisor or Google can help you gauge the quality and service of your accommodation.
- **Flexibility:** If you're traveling during the off-season (April-May or September-November), you may find better deals and availability with flexible dates.

Peru offers a wide range of accommodations to suit every budget and preference. From luxurious hotels to eco-conscious retreats and budget-friendly hostels, there's something for everyone. With the right accommodation, your stay in Peru can be both comfortable and memorable, providing you with a true sense of the country's unique culture and natural beauty.

Chapter 6: Peruvian Culture & Etiquette

Peru is a country where ancient traditions, colonial influences, and diverse indigenous cultures blend to create a vibrant and unique cultural identity. From the legacy of the Inca Empire to contemporary Peru, the country's cultural richness is evident in its art, food, architecture, festivals, and daily customs. This chapter provides a comprehensive overview of the key cultural elements in Peru, from social customs and etiquette to language, communication styles, and the best practices for respecting local traditions.

6.1 Understanding Peru's Cultural Heritage

Peru is a nation with a deep and multifaceted cultural heritage, shaped by thousands of years of history. Ancient civilizations such as the Incas, along with Spanish colonial influence and the contributions of Afro-Peruvian and Asian communities, have all played a role in forming the modern-day culture of Peru.

- **Incan Legacy:**
  The Inca Empire, one of the largest and most advanced civilizations of pre-Columbian America, left a lasting influence on Peru. Iconic landmarks like Machu Picchu, as well as advanced agricultural techniques and complex social structures, are a testament to their legacy.
- **Indigenous Traditions:**
  Peru's indigenous groups, including the Quechua, Aymara, Ashaninka, and many others, maintain rich traditions in language, art, music, and community practices. These indigenous cultures are a vibrant part of the country's identity, especially in regions like the Sacred Valley and Lake Titicaca.
- **Colonial Influence:**
  After Spanish colonization in the 16th century, Peru adopted many European customs, including Christianity, as well as architectural styles seen in the colonial cities like Lima and Cusco. The fusion of European and indigenous traditions created the unique Peruvian culture we see today.
- **Afro-Peruvian Heritage:**
  African slaves brought to Peru during the colonial period also left a

significant cultural imprint, especially in coastal regions. Afro-Peruvian music, dance, and cuisine are important elements of Peru's cultural identity.

Cultural Heritage Highlights:

- **Machu Picchu:** One of the world's most famous archaeological sites, embodying the majesty of the Inca civilization.
- **Cusco:** The historic heart of the Inca Empire, filled with ancient ruins and colonial architecture.
- **Traditional Peruvian Textiles:** Known for their intricate patterns and vibrant colors, indigenous weavers in Peru continue to create world-renowned textiles.
- **Afro-Peruvian Music:** Rhythms such as those from the *cajón* (wooden drum) are an essential part of Peru's musical culture.

6.2 Social Etiquette & Customs

When traveling through Peru, understanding local customs and etiquette will help you connect with locals and show respect for their traditions. Peruvians are generally friendly, polite, and hospitable, but they appreciate travelers who take the time to learn and follow social norms.

- **Greetings:**
  The typical greeting in Peru is a handshake, accompanied by eye contact and a friendly smile. In more informal settings, especially among friends or close acquaintances, it is common to exchange a kiss on the right cheek.
- **Respect for Elders:**
  Family is central to Peruvian society, and respect for older individuals is highly valued. It's important to use formal titles like *Señor* (Mr.) or *Señora* (Mrs.) when addressing older people, particularly in rural areas.
- **Personal Space:**
  Peruvians are known for being warm and affectionate, and they may stand closer to one another when conversing than people from some Western cultures are accustomed to. Don't be surprised if personal space is more limited in social situations.

- **Politeness in Conversation:**
  Peruvian culture tends to avoid confrontational or direct speech. People often express their opinions with more subtlety, and it's common to hear phrases like *quizá* (maybe) or *tal vez* (perhaps) rather than a definitive "no." Being polite, patient, and indirect in communication is appreciated.
- **Gift-Giving:**
  Bringing small gifts when visiting someone's home is a nice gesture, particularly if you're invited for a meal. Suitable gifts include flowers, handicrafts, or locally produced food or drink items. Avoid overly extravagant gifts, as they might make the host uncomfortable.

Social Etiquette Highlights:

- Handshakes are standard greetings, but cheek kissing is common among friends and family.
- Show respect for older people, especially in rural areas, by using formal titles.
- Be mindful of personal space—Peruvians tend to stand close during conversations.

6.3 Language & Communication: Spanish and Quechua

While Spanish is the dominant language in Peru, the country is also home to a significant number of indigenous languages. Understanding the basics of these languages can deepen your cultural experience.

- **Spanish:**
  Spanish is spoken throughout Peru, especially in major cities like Lima, Arequipa, and Cusco. The accent is clear and relatively neutral, although regional variations and unique Peruvian words exist. Many Peruvians are bilingual and also speak their indigenous languages.
- **Quechua:**
  As the language of the Inca Empire, Quechua remains widely spoken, especially in rural Andean regions such as Cusco, Puno, and the Sacred Valley. Quechua is a key part of the region's cultural identity, and many people continue to speak it at home and in their communities.

- **Aymara:**
  Aymara is another important indigenous language spoken in the southern Andes, particularly around Lake Titicaca. Although fewer people speak Aymara than Quechua, it still plays a vital role in the cultural practices of the region.
- **Communication Style:**
  Peruvians tend to be more indirect and polite in their communication compared to people from some Western cultures. They may avoid bluntly saying "no" and instead use expressions like *quizá* (maybe) or *tal vez* (perhaps) to soften their responses.

Language Highlights:

- **Basic Quechua Words:**
  - *Ñawi* = Eye
  - *Wasi* = House
  - *Inti* = Sun
- **Useful Spanish Phrases:**
  - "¿Cuánto cuesta?" = How much is it?
  - "¿Dónde está...?" = Where is...?
  - "Gracias" = Thank you

6.4 Tipping Practices

Tipping in Peru is generally expected in service industries, though it's not mandatory. Leaving tips is a way to show appreciation for good service, especially in tourist areas.

- **Restaurants:**
  Many restaurants include a service charge (typically 10-15%) in the bill, but if it's not included, a 10% tip is customary. In more casual settings, rounding up the bill or leaving small change is also appreciated.
- **Hotels:**
  Tipping hotel staff is a kind gesture. It's typical to leave a tip of about **S/5-10** per day for housekeeping and **S/5 per bag** for porters.

- **Taxis & Rideshares:**
  While tipping taxi drivers is not obligatory, rounding up the fare is appreciated. For rideshare services like Uber, tips are optional but welcome for exceptional service.
- **Tour Guides:**
  For guided tours, it's customary to tip your guide **S/20-50** per day, depending on the length and quality of the tour, while drivers generally receive **S/10-20**.

6.5 What to Wear

Peru's diverse climate means that what you wear will depend on where you are traveling. From the coastal cities to the highlands and the Amazon jungle, you'll need to pack accordingly.

- **Lima & Coastal Areas:**
  Lima and the coastal cities have mild, temperate weather. Light, comfortable clothing is suitable for most of the year, but evenings can be cool, so bringing a light jacket or sweater is recommended.
- **Andean Highlands & Sacred Valley:**
  The highlands, including Cusco and Machu Picchu, can be chilly, especially at night. Layered clothing is ideal—pack a warm jacket, gloves, and comfortable walking shoes. Be prepared for sudden temperature changes, particularly if you're visiting the mountains.
- **Amazon Jungle:**
  The Amazon region is hot, humid, and rainy year-round. Wear light, moisture-wicking clothes to stay cool, and long sleeves and pants to protect yourself from insects. Don't forget to bring insect repellent and a rain jacket.

Packing Tips:

- **Layering is Key:** High-altitude areas like Cusco can be cold, while lowland areas like the Amazon are hot and humid.
- **Comfortable Footwear:** You'll do a lot of walking, so sturdy shoes are essential.

- **Sun Protection:** The sun can be intense at high altitudes, so pack sunscreen, a hat, and sunglasses.

6.6 Celebrations & Festivals

Peru's festivals are an expression of the country's cultural diversity, often blending indigenous and Catholic traditions. The celebrations, which vary by region, offer a fantastic opportunity to experience the country's music, dance, and religious customs.

- **Inti Raymi (Festival of the Sun):**
  Held on June 24 in Cusco, this festival celebrates the winter solstice and honors Inti, the Inca sun god. It features grand reenactments of ancient rituals, vibrant parades, and ceremonies at key Inca sites.
- **Fiesta de la Virgen de la Candelaria:**
  One of the largest religious festivals in South America, the Candelaria Festival takes place every February in Puno. It honors the Virgin of Candelaria with parades, music, and traditional dances.
- **Semana Santa (Holy Week):**
  During Easter week, Peru comes alive with religious processions and cultural events. Cusco's Semana Santa is especially notable, with a fusion of Inca and Catholic traditions seen in the many parades and processions.
- **Carnaval:**
  Carnival is a nationwide celebration held in February, with music, dance, and street parties filling the streets. It's particularly lively in Cajamarca, Puno, and other regions.

Chapter 7: Cuisine & Dining

Peruvian cuisine is a vibrant fusion of flavors, showcasing the country's rich history and diverse geography. From coastal seafood dishes like *ceviche* to hearty Andean stews, food is a key part of Peru's identity. The influence of indigenous ingredients, Spanish colonization, and immigrant cultures from Asia and Africa make Peruvian dishes unique and varied. This chapter explores the essential components of Peru's culinary scene, including must-try dishes, dining etiquette, street food, and vegetarian options. Whether you're enjoying a meal at a high-end restaurant or grabbing a snack from a street vendor, Peru offers a wealth of flavors to explore.

7.1 The Flavors of Peru: A Culinary Overview

Peruvian cuisine is globally recognized for its complexity and diversity. Rooted in indigenous ingredients like *potatoes, corn, quinoa,* and *chili peppers,* Peru's food also reflects the colonial legacy and immigrant influence from Asia, Europe, and Africa. Each region of Peru offers distinct flavors, with the highland Andes focusing on grains and potatoes, the coast emphasizing fresh seafood, and the jungle offering exotic fruits and Amazonian ingredients.

- **Andean Ingredients:**
  The highlands are home to potatoes (over 3,000 varieties), quinoa, *kiwicha* (amaranth), and *chuño* (freeze-dried potatoes), which have been part of Peru's diet for thousands of years.
- **Coastal Influences:**
  Peru's long coastline brings fresh seafood into everyday meals, such as *ceviche* (raw fish cured in citrus juices) and various fish-based stews.
- **Amazonian Flavors:**
  The Amazonian region adds tropical fruits and unique jungle ingredients like *camu camu, aguaje,* and *bacaba* to the culinary mix. Local staples like *yuca, plantains,* and jungle meats also make appearances in traditional dishes.

Key Culinary Highlights:

- **Ceviche:** Fresh fish marinated in citrus juices and complemented by onions, cilantro, and chili peppers.

- **Lomo Saltado:** A flavorful stir-fry combining beef, onions, tomatoes, and French fries served with rice.
- **Pisco Sour:** Peru's signature cocktail made with Pisco, lime juice, egg white, and bitters.

7.2 Must-Try Peruvian Dishes

Peruvian cuisine offers a variety of flavors, from fresh seafood to comforting stews. Here are some dishes you shouldn't miss during your visit:

- **Ceviche (S/ 25-45):**
  A popular dish along the coast, *ceviche* consists of raw fish marinated in lime juice, chili, and onions, typically served with corn and sweet potato. It's an absolute must-try, especially in Lima.
  Where to Try:
    - *La Mar* (Lima)
    - *Pescados Capitales* (Cusco)
    - *El Mercado* (Lima)
- **Lomo Saltado (S/ 30-50):**
  A fusion of Chinese and Peruvian cooking, *lomo saltado* features stir-fried beef with onions, tomatoes, and French fries, served with rice. It's a hearty, savory dish available throughout Peru.
  Where to Try:
    - *Astrid y Gastón* (Lima)
    - *Pescados Capitales* (Cusco)
- **Aji de Gallina (S/ 30-40):**
  A rich chicken stew with a creamy sauce made from *aji amarillo* (yellow chili), garlic, nuts, and cheese, traditionally served with rice and potatoes.
  Where to Try:
    - *El Rinconcito de la Abuela* (Lima)
    - *Lima 27* (Lima)
- **Causa Rellena (S/ 20-35):**
  A layered potato dish, typically filled with tuna, chicken, or avocado, and served cold. It's a refreshing dish, perfect for warm weather.
  Where to Try:

- ○ *La Lucha Sangucheria* (Lima)
- ○ *El Rincón de la Abuela* (Cusco)
- **Pisco Sour (S/ 20-30):**
  Peru's national cocktail, made from Pisco, lime juice, egg white, and bitters.
  It's a perfect drink to enjoy before a meal or as a nightcap.
  Where to Try:
  - ○ *Bar Pescados Capitales* (Lima)
  - ○ *Hotel Bolivar* (Lima)

7.3 Street Food Culture

Street food is an essential part of Peru's food scene, offering affordable, authentic tastes of local flavors. From grilled *anticuchos* to fried *empanadas*, the streets of Lima, Cusco, and Arequipa are filled with food vendors offering quick, satisfying meals.

- **Anticuchos (S/ 5-10):**
  Skewered beef heart, marinated and grilled, often served with potatoes and corn. This dish is especially popular in Lima's *Miraflores* and *Barranco* districts.
- **Churros (S/ 3-5):**
  Fried dough pastries filled with caramel, chocolate, or sugar, served as a sweet snack in markets and food stalls.
- **Tamales (S/ 5-10):**
  Steamed corn dough, filled with meat, cheese, or olives and wrapped in a banana leaf. Tamales are common in the Andean regions of Cusco and Puno.

Top Street Food Spots:

- **Barranco (Lima):** Known for its trendy cafes and street food vendors.
- **Miraflores (Lima):** Especially around Parque Kennedy, vendors offer *anticuchos* and other local treats.
- **Surquillo Market (Lima):** A bustling market known for fresh seafood and traditional street food.

7.4 Food Markets & Where to Eat

Markets in Peru offer a window into local culinary traditions. From fresh produce to ready-to-eat meals, these markets are great places to discover the heart of Peru's food culture.

- **Mercado de San Pedro (Cusco):**
  One of the largest and most popular markets in Peru, it's packed with fresh produce, meats, cheeses, and local specialties. Don't miss the *chicharrón* (fried pork) and *anticuchos* stalls.
- **Mercado de Surquillo (Lima):**
  A local market where you can find fresh seafood, meats, and vegetables, as well as dishes like *ceviche* and *pisco sours*. It's a great place to immerse yourself in the daily rhythms of Lima.
- **Mercado Central (Lima):**
  Located in downtown Lima, this market is a great spot to try a variety of traditional Peruvian dishes, from *pisco sours* to *ceviche*.

7.5 Dining Etiquette & Tips

When dining in Peru, it's important to follow a few local customs to fully embrace the cultural experience:

- **Meal Times:**
  - **Desayuno (Breakfast):** A light meal, often consisting of bread, cheese, and coffee or tea.
  - **Almuerzo (Lunch):** The main meal of the day, typically served between 1:00 PM and 3:00 PM.
  - **Cena (Dinner):** A lighter meal, often served later in the evening around 7:00 PM to 9:00 PM.
- **Etiquette:**
  - Wait for your host to start eating before beginning your meal.
  - If service charges are not included, a 10% tip is customary.
- **Drinking Etiquette:**
  When toasting with *pisco sours* or beer, it's customary to make eye contact and say "¡Salud!" (To your health!).

7.6 Vegan & Vegetarian Options

Peru is a fantastic destination for vegetarians and vegans, with a wide variety of plant-based foods available. Many traditional dishes can be made vegan or vegetarian, and restaurants across major cities offer plant-based versions of classic Peruvian meals.

- **Vegan & Vegetarian Dishes:**
    - **Quinoa Soup (S/ 12-20):** A nutritious and flavorful soup made with quinoa and vegetables.
    - **Lentil Stew (S/ 15-25):** A hearty stew made with lentils, vegetables, and Andean spices.
    - **Papas a la Huancaína (S/ 15-25):** A potato dish with a creamy, vegan-friendly sauce made from *aji amarillo* (yellow chili).
- **Top Vegan & Vegetarian Restaurants:**
    - **Veda (Lima):** A modern restaurant offering plant-based versions of traditional dishes.
    - **Green Point (Cusco):** A vegan restaurant with a wide variety of traditional and fusion dishes.
    - **El Vegetariano (Arequipa):** A popular spot for vegetarians and vegans in Arequipa.

Peru's diverse and rich culinary traditions provide a flavorful journey for travelers. Whether you're enjoying a street snack, indulging in a multi-course meal, or sipping a *pisco sour*, the food in Peru is as diverse and captivating as the country itself.

Chapter 8: Attractions & Activities

Peru is a country of remarkable contrasts, where ancient cultures coexist with breathtaking natural beauty. Whether you're interested in exploring ancient ruins, immersing yourself in indigenous traditions, or seeking thrilling outdoor adventures, Peru has something for every traveler. From the iconic Machu Picchu to the exotic Amazon rainforest, the country's attractions promise unforgettable experiences. In this chapter, we'll explore the must-see destinations and activities across Peru, offering practical details on locations, pricing, and booking tips to help you plan your journey.

8.1 Lima: The Capital City

Lima, the vibrant capital of Peru, is a city of fascinating contrasts. It offers everything from historical sites and colonial-era architecture to modern malls and lively coastal neighborhoods. Lima serves as the country's primary gateway and is a must-visit for those seeking a taste of Peru's urban and cultural dynamism.

- **Plaza Mayor (Main Square):**

Lima's historic center, where you'll find the *Catedral de Lima* and *Palacio de Gobierno* (Government Palace). The square is a UNESCO World Heritage site and an excellent place to start your exploration of the city.

Entry: Free to explore the plaza; museum and church entry fees range from S/ 10-20.

Location: Central Lima, Jirón de la Unión.

- **Miraflores:**

A trendy district known for its upscale shopping, beautiful parks, and stunning views of the Pacific Ocean. Visit *Parque Kennedy* and *Parque del Amor* for panoramic vistas.

Highlight: Enjoy the dramatic coastal cliffs and vibrant urban atmosphere.

Entry: Free to explore; museums and ruins such as *Huaca Pucllana* (S/ 12-30).

Location: Miraflores District.

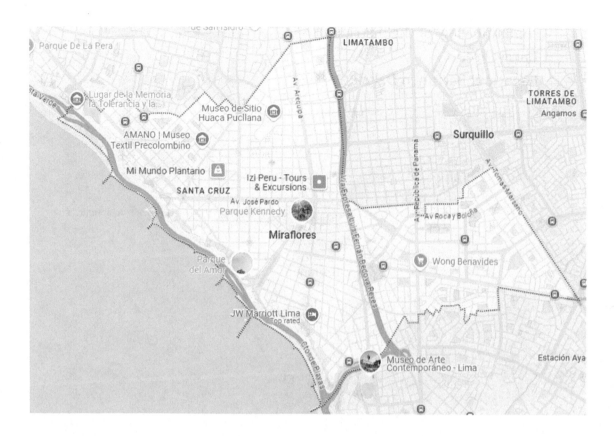

- **Barranco:**

A charming bohemian neighborhood renowned for its art scene, colorful murals, and cozy cafés. The *Puente de los Suspiros* (Bridge of Sighs) offers a romantic view of the district.

Entry: Free.

Location: Barranco District.

- **Museo Larco:**

A must-see for art and history enthusiasts, Museo Larco houses an impressive collection of pre-Columbian artifacts, including ancient textiles, pottery, and gold pieces.

Entry: S/ 35

Location: Av. Bolívar 1515, Pueblo Libre.

Website: https://www.museolarco.org

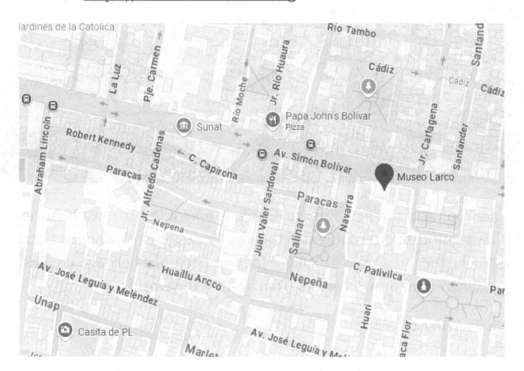

8.2 Cusco: Gateway to the Sacred Valley

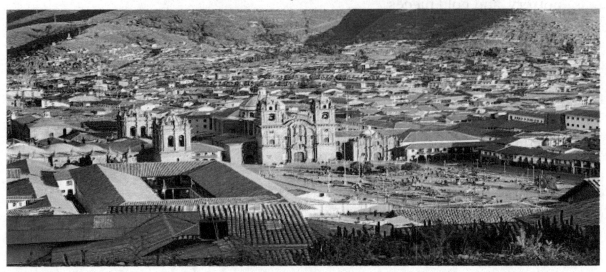

As the former capital of the Inca Empire, Cusco is one of Peru's most historically and culturally significant cities. It is also the ideal base for exploring the Sacred Valley and Machu Picchu. Cusco's blend of Inca and colonial heritage creates a unique atmosphere that draws visitors from around the world.

- **Plaza de Armas:**

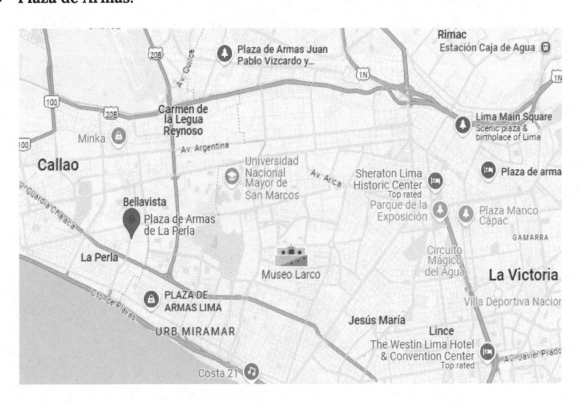

The main square of Cusco, surrounded by colonial buildings, churches, and bustling cafés, is the center of life in the city.

Entry: Free

Location: Central Cusco.

- **Sacsayhuamán:**

  This impressive Inca archaeological site features massive stone walls and offers sweeping views of the city below. The site was once a key religious and ceremonial center for the Incas.

  Entry: S/ 70 (Boleto Turístico - Tourist Ticket).

  Location: 10 minutes from Cusco city center.

- **Qorikancha (Temple of the Sun):**

  Once the richest and most important temple in the Inca Empire, Qorikancha now stands as a fusion of Inca and colonial architecture, housing a fascinating museum.

  Entry: S/ 15

  Location: Av. El Sol, Cusco.

8.3 Machu Picchu: Lost City of the Incas

Machu Picchu, the Lost City of the Incas, is one of the most iconic archaeological sites in the world. Nestled high in the Andes Mountains, this ancient Inca citadel is a UNESCO World Heritage site and a must-visit for anyone traveling to Peru.

- **Trekking to Machu Picchu:**
  The classic Inca Trail trek is the most popular route to Machu Picchu, but there are also alternative treks like the Salkantay and Lares treks. Each offers its own unique experience, with stunning landscapes and historical sites along the way.
  Price: Inca Trail permits range from S/ 300-600, depending on the route.
  Best Time to Visit: Dry season (April to October).
  Booking: Inca Trail Permits
- **Machu Picchu Citadel:**
  Explore the ancient ruins of Machu Picchu, including highlights such as the *Intihuatana* stone (the Inca sun dial), the *Temple of the Sun*, and the *Room of the Three Windows*.
  Entry Fee: S/ 152
  Location: Aguas Calientes (take a train from Cusco and a 30-minute bus ride to the site).

8.4 Sacred Valley: Ollantaytambo, Pisac, and More

The Sacred Valley is home to a series of impressive Inca ruins, vibrant markets, and stunning landscapes. It's a key part of any trip to Cusco and provides valuable insights into Inca culture.

- **Ollantaytambo:**

A scenic town with impressive Inca ruins, Ollantaytambo was once an important military and religious center. The site features terraces, temples, and a ceremonial center.

Entry Fee: S/ 70 (Boleto Turístico).

Location: 1.5 hours from Cusco.

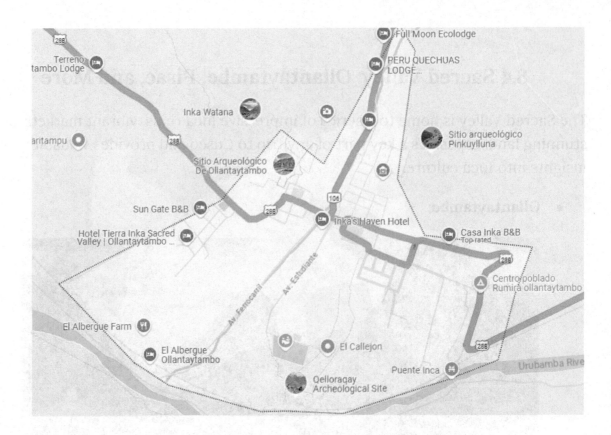

- **Pisac:**

Known for its terraced agricultural ruins and the famous Pisac Market, where visitors can purchase traditional handicrafts.

Entry Fee: S/ 70

Location: 45 minutes from Cusco.

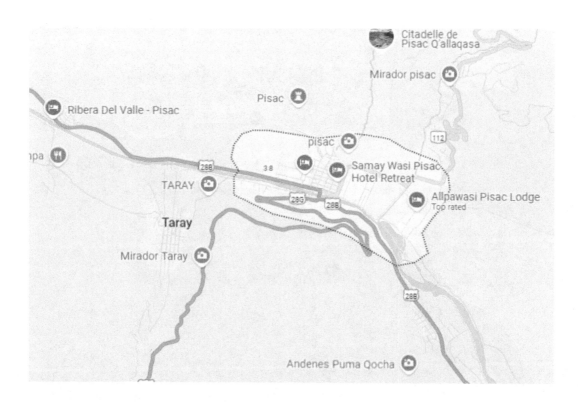

- **Chinchero:**

A small village known for its well-preserved Inca terraces and colonial church. It's an excellent place to learn about traditional weaving techniques from local artisans.

Entry Fee: S/ 10

Location: 30 minutes from Cusco.

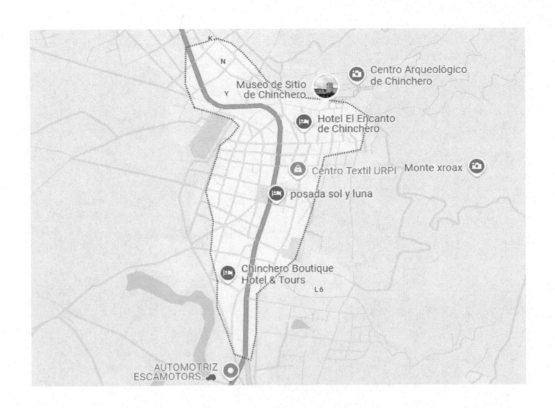

8.5 The Nazca Lines

The Nazca Lines, one of Peru's most enigmatic landmarks, are a series of large geoglyphs etched into the desert floor. These ancient designs, which depict animals, plants, and geometric shapes, are best viewed from the air.

- **Flight Over the Nazca Lines:**
  The most popular way to see the Nazca Lines is by taking a small plane flight over the desert.
  Price: S/ 350-500 for a 30-minute flight.
  Location: Nazca, about 7 hours south of Lima by bus.
  Website: https://www.aeroparacas.com

8.6 Lake Titicaca: Floating Islands & Indigenous Cultures

Lake Titicaca, the world's highest navigable lake, sits on the border between Peru and Bolivia. It is home to indigenous communities who still live on the famous floating reed islands, maintaining traditional ways of life.

- **Uros Floating Islands:**

These artificial islands, made from *totora* reeds, are inhabited by the Uros people, who craft boats and homes from the same material.
Price: S/ 20-30 for a boat tour.
Location: 30-minute boat ride from Puno.

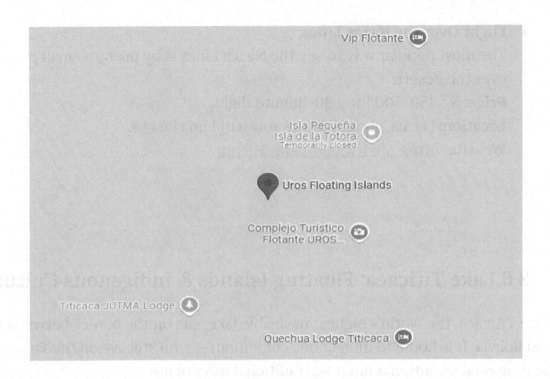

- **Taquile Island:**

Known for its exquisite textiles and traditional lifestyle, Taquile Island offers hikes with scenic views and opportunities to engage with local residents.
Price: S/ 50 for a guided tour.
Location: 2-3 hours by boat from Puno.

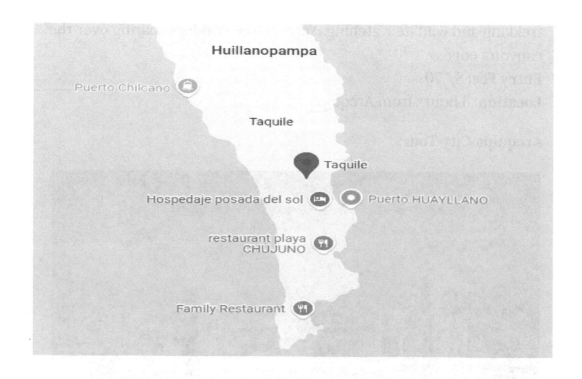

8.7 Arequipa & the Colca Canyon

Arequipa, known as the "White City" for its colonial buildings made of volcanic rock, is the gateway to Colca Canyon, home to the Andean condor and some of the deepest canyons in the world.

- **Colca Canyon:**

One of the deepest canyons in the world, Colca Canyon is a great spot for

trekking and wildlife watching. You can see condors soaring over the canyon's edge.
Entry Fee: S/ 70
Location: 3 hours from Arequipa.

- **Arequipa City Tour:**

Explore Arequipa's beautiful *Santa Catalina Monastery* and *Plaza de Armas*, both of which are steeped in colonial history.
Entry Fee: S/ 35 for the monastery.
Location: Arequipa city center.

8.8 The Amazon Jungle: Iquitos & Puerto Maldonado

The Amazon rainforest is a vast, biodiverse region, and Peru offers two main access points for exploring this pristine wilderness—Puerto Maldonado and Iquitos.

- **Iquitos:**
  This isolated city, accessible only by air or river, is the gateway to the northern Amazon, offering boat tours, wildlife excursions, and cultural experiences.

Price: Tours range from S/ 150-500 for 1-3 day jungle tours.
Location: Iquitos, accessible by flight from Lima.

- **Puerto Maldonado:**

  Known for eco-lodges and wildlife tours, Puerto Maldonado offers access to the Tambopata National Reserve and *Lake Sandoval*.
  Price: Tours range from S/ 200-700.
  Location: Puerto Maldonado, 1-hour flight from Cusco.

8.9 Paracas & the Ballestas Islands

The coastal region of Paracas is home to the Ballestas Islands, where visitors can spot sea lions, penguins, and a variety of bird species.

- **Ballestas Islands Boat Tour:**

A popular 2-hour boat tour takes you to the Ballestas Islands, often called the "Poor Man's Galapagos," to observe the incredible wildlife.
Price: S/ 40-70
Location: Paracas, 3-4 hours south of Lima.

8.10 Adventure Activities: Trekking, Surfing, and Sandboarding

Peru is an adventurer's paradise, with activities for all levels of thrill-seekers.

- **Trekking:**
  From the *Inca Trail* to alternative treks like the *Salkantay* and *Lares* treks, there's a wealth of hiking opportunities across the Andes.
  Price: Multi-day treks range from S/ 500-1,000.
- **Surfing:**
  Peru's northern coast, especially *Máncora* and *Huanchaco*, is known for world-class surf breaks.
  Price: Surfboard rentals range from S/ 30-60 per day.
- **Sandboarding in Huacachina:**
  Ride the dunes on a sandboard or take a thrilling dune buggy ride in the desert oasis of Huacachina.
  Price: S/ 50-80 for a half-day tour.
  Location: Huacachina, near Ica.

Peru's rich history and stunning landscapes offer an array of experiences, from high-altitude treks to rainforest explorations and desert adventures. With a diverse range of attractions, there's something for every type of traveler to explore.

Chapter 9: Outdoor Adventures

Peru is an adventurer's paradise, offering an array of outdoor experiences that are as diverse as the country's landscapes. Whether you're trekking the ancient Inca Trail to Machu Picchu, exploring the jungles of the Amazon Rainforest, paragliding over the Pacific coast, or surfing world-class waves, Peru delivers unforgettable adventures. This chapter explores the top outdoor activities across the country, including pricing, locations, and useful tips to enhance your experience.

9.1 Trekking to Machu Picchu

Trekking to Machu Picchu is one of the most iconic outdoor activities in the world. The journey to this ancient Inca city can be achieved through several treks, each offering unique views and experiences of the Andean landscape.

Inca Trail:

- **Overview:** The 4-day Inca Trail trek is the most popular route, taking hikers through diverse ecosystems, Inca ruins, and scenic vistas. The trek culminates in a sunrise arrival at the Sun Gate, where visitors get their first breathtaking view of Machu Picchu.
- **Difficulty:** Moderate, with altitude challenges and uneven terrain.
- **Price:** $200-300 USD (approx. S/ 700-1,000), depending on the tour operator. It is advisable to book 4-6 months in advance due to permit limitations.
- **Location:** The trek starts at *Km 82* along the train tracks, a 1.5-hour drive from Cusco.
- **Website for bookings & permits:** Inca Trail Permits

Alternative Treks to Machu Picchu: For those seeking a less crowded trek or a different adventure, Peru offers several alternative routes to Machu Picchu.

- **Salkantay Trek:**
  - **Overview:** This 5-day trek takes you through high-altitude landscapes, past glaciers, waterfalls, and lush tropical forests. The Salkantay Trek is ideal for those looking for a more challenging route.

- **Difficulty:** Challenging (altitudes up to 4,600 meters).
- **Price:** $300-500 USD (approx. S/ 1,000-1,800).
- **Location:** Begins at *Mollepata*, 3 hours from Cusco.
- **Website for bookings:** Salkantay Trekking
- **Lares Trek:**
    - **Overview:** The Lares Trek is a 3-4 day route that is less crowded and offers a more cultural experience, with visits to remote Andean villages and opportunities to interact with local communities.
    - **Difficulty:** Moderate.
    - **Price:** $200-350 USD (approx. S/ 700-1,200).
    - **Location:** Begins in the *Lares Valley*, 3 hours from Cusco.
    - **Website for bookings:** Lares Treks

9.2 Inca Trail vs. Alternative Treks

Choosing the right trek depends on your preferences. Here's a comparison of the classic Inca Trail and the alternative routes:

Route	Duration	Difficulty	Highlights	Best For
Inca Trail	4 days	Moderate	Iconic Inca ruins, high-altitude views	History buffs, iconic views
Salkantay Trek	5 days	Challenging	Glaciers, waterfalls, scenic vistas	Adventurers, high-altitude trekkers
Lares Trek	3-4 days	Moderate	Andean villages, local culture	Cultural immersion seekers

9.3 Hiking in the Andes

The Andes mountain range stretches across Peru and offers some of the best hiking experiences in the world. From shorter day hikes to multi-day treks, these mountains provide incredible views, ancient ruins, and rich cultural encounters.

Rainbow Mountain (Vinicunca):

- **Overview:** A popular 1-day trek to the stunning Rainbow Mountain, known for its vibrant, multi-colored slopes caused by mineral deposits.
- **Difficulty:** Moderate (3-4 hours of hiking at high altitudes).
- **Price:** $30-50 USD (S/ 100-150), with guided tours including transportation and meals.
- **Location:** 3 hours from Cusco.
- **Website for bookings:** https://www.perurail.com

Huchuy Qosqo Trek:

- **Overview:** A 2-day trek that combines beautiful mountain landscapes with a visit to the ancient Inca site of Huchuy Qosqo, where you can explore the ruins and learn about local history.
- **Difficulty:** Moderate.
- **Price:** $90-150 USD (S/ 300-500).
- **Location:** Starts at the town of *Tauca*, 1 hour from Cusco.
- **Website for bookings:** https://www.peruviantravelsolutions.com

9.4 The Amazon Rainforest: Exploration & Wildlife Tours

The Amazon Rainforest in Peru is one of the most biodiverse ecosystems on Earth. Visiting this lush, vibrant environment is a once-in-a-lifetime opportunity for nature lovers and wildlife enthusiasts.

Iquitos Amazon Tours:

- **Overview:** Iquitos is the main gateway to the Peruvian Amazon, and from here, you can take boat tours to explore the rainforest and spot wildlife such as monkeys, sloths, and exotic birds.

- **Price:** $100-300 USD (S/ 350-1,000) for multi-day guided tours.
- **Location:** Iquitos, 1.5-hour flight from Lima.
- **Website for bookings:** https://www.peruamazontravel.com

Puerto Maldonado & Tambopata Reserve:

- **Overview:** Located in southeastern Peru, Puerto Maldonado is the gateway to the Tambopata National Reserve, known for its rich wildlife, including jaguars, macaws, and caimans.
- **Price:** $150-500 USD (S/ 500-1,800) for 2-3 day tours.
- **Location:** 1-hour flight from Cusco.
- **Website for tours:** https://www.jungletoursperu.com

9.5 Paragliding in Lima

For those seeking an exhilarating adventure, paragliding in Lima offers the chance to soar over the Pacific Ocean, enjoying spectacular views of the city's cliffs and coastline.

- **Overview:** Paragliding in Lima's Miraflores district is an incredible way to experience the city from above. Flights are conducted by experienced pilots and typically last around 15-20 minutes.
- **Price:** $60-120 USD (S/ 200-400) for a tandem flight.
- **Location:** Miraflores, near the *Cliffs of Miraflores*.
- **Website for bookings:** https://www.parapentelima.com

9.6 Water Sports & Coastal Adventures

Peru's coastline stretches for over 2,400 kilometers, offering a range of thrilling water-based activities such as surfing, kayaking, and sandboarding. Whether you're an experienced surfer or a beginner, Peru's beaches provide perfect conditions.

Surfing in Máncora & Huanchaco:

- **Overview:** The northern coast of Peru, particularly *Máncora* and *Huanchaco*, is renowned for its consistent waves, making it a top surfing destination.
- **Price:** $30-60 USD (S/ 100-200) per day for surfboard rentals. Surf lessons typically cost $50-70 USD (S/ 180-250).
- **Location:** Máncora and Huanchaco.
- **Website for rentals & lessons:** https://www.mancorasurf.com

Sandboarding & Dune Buggy Tours in Huacachina:

- **Overview:** Located in the desert oasis of Huacachina, just outside of Ica, you can take a thrilling dune buggy ride and try sandboarding down the massive dunes.
- **Price:** $15-25 USD (S/ 50-80) for a half-day tour.
- **Location:** Huacachina, near Ica, 5 hours south of Lima.
- **Website for bookings:** https://www.huacachina.com

Kayaking in Paracas:

- **Overview:** Explore the Paracas National Reserve by kayak, where you can spot sea lions, pelicans, and other marine wildlife while paddling along the coast.
- **Price:** $12-20 USD (S/ 40-60) per hour.
- **Location:** Paracas, 3-4 hours south of Lima.
- **Website for rentals:** https://www.paracasadventure.com

Chapter 10: Shopping & Souvenirs

Peru offers a vibrant array of shopping experiences where you can find everything from handmade crafts to colorful textiles and one-of-a-kind jewelry. The country's rich cultural heritage is reflected in the unique items you can purchase, making them memorable souvenirs from your travels. In this chapter, we explore the best places to shop, the types of traditional crafts you can expect, and ethical shopping practices that support local communities.

10.1 Best Markets & Shopping Districts

Peru's markets are lively hubs, offering a vast range of products from fresh produce to handmade goods. Visiting these markets gives you a deeper insight into the country's culture while finding the perfect souvenir.

- **Mercado de San Pedro (Cusco):**
  - **Overview:** One of Cusco's oldest and most famous markets, Mercado de San Pedro is a great place to find local food, textiles, and handicrafts.
  - **Location:** Av. San Pedro, Cusco.
  - **Highlights:** Fresh produce, cheeses, colorful textiles, and artisanal crafts.
  - **Website:** https://www.cusco.travel
- **Mercado de las Brujas (Lima):**
  - **Overview:** Known as the "Witches' Market," this market in Lima specializes in Andean spiritual items, including healing herbs, charms, and mystical artifacts.
  - **Location:** Jirón de la Unión, Lima.
  - **Highlights:** Spiritual items, mystical charms, and Andean crafts.
  - **Website:** https://www.peru.travel
- **Pisac Market (Sacred Valley):**
  - **Overview:** Held every Sunday, the Pisac market offers a rich collection of local crafts, textiles, and jewelry, perfect for souvenir hunting.
  - **Location:** Pisac, Sacred Valley (approximately 45 minutes from Cusco).
  - **Highlights:** Traditional garments, pottery, and unique jewelry.

- **Website:** https://www.peru.travel

10.2 Handicrafts & Indigenous Art

Peru is renowned for its traditional handicrafts that are deeply rooted in indigenous cultures. Many of these crafts are passed down through generations and reflect the unique artistry of the different regions.

- **Ceramics:**
  - **Overview:** Peruvian ceramics, especially from the Nazca and highland regions, feature intricate designs with traditional symbols and motifs.
  - **Where to Buy:** Pisac, Cusco, Arequipa.
  - **Price Range:** $5-30 USD (S/ 20-100).
- **Wood Carvings:**
  - **Overview:** Hand-carved wooden pieces, such as masks and figurines, often depict animals and indigenous deities, making them a great cultural souvenir.
  - **Where to Buy:** Sacred Valley, Ayacucho.
  - **Price Range:** $10-50 USD (S/ 30-150).

10.3 Textiles: Alpaca Wool & Peruvian Weaving

Peru is world-famous for its alpaca wool, known for its softness, warmth, and durability. The textiles produced from alpaca wool are both functional and artistic, with patterns that have cultural significance.

- **Alpaca Wool Products:**
  - **Overview:** Alpaca wool items like scarves, sweaters, and blankets are crafted in highland cities such as Arequipa and Cusco. These items are known for their warmth and high quality.
  - **Where to Buy:** Cusco, Arequipa, Lima.
  - **Price Range:** $15-100 USD (S/ 50-350).
  - **Website:** https://www.perualpaca.com

- **Handwoven Textiles:**
  - **Overview:** Traditional Andean textiles, including ponchos and blankets, are made by hand using techniques that date back to the Incas. These pieces often feature vibrant colors and geometric patterns.
  - **Where to Buy:** Sacred Valley, Puno.
  - **Price Range:** $20-150 USD (S/ 70-500).

10.4 Local Art and Jewelry

Peru's art scene, deeply influenced by its indigenous culture, offers a variety of unique art pieces, from paintings to intricate silver jewelry. Many of these works are inspired by the country's history and natural beauty.

- **Silver Jewelry:**
  - **Overview:** Peru is famous for its high-quality silver jewelry, often adorned with vibrant semi-precious stones like turquoise and lapis lazuli.
  - **Where to Buy:** Cusco, Lima, Arequipa.
  - **Price Range:** $20-200 USD (S/ 70-700).
  - **Website:** https://www.peru-jewelry.com
- **Paintings and Artwork:**
  - **Overview:** Many local artists create paintings and art that reflect Peruvian landscapes, folklore, and ancient traditions, making them excellent and meaningful souvenirs.
  - **Where to Buy:** Art galleries in Cusco, Lima, Arequipa.
  - **Price Range:** $30-500 USD (S/ 100-1,800).

10.5 Ethical Souvenirs: Supporting Local Communities

When purchasing souvenirs in Peru, it's important to consider the ethical implications of your purchases. Supporting local artisans through fair-trade shops ensures that your money goes directly to the makers, helping sustain traditional craftsmanship and improve local livelihoods.

- **Fair-Trade Crafts:**
  - **Overview:** Many fair-trade stores and cooperatives offer products made by artisans who are paid fairly for their work, ensuring the sustainability of their craft.
  - **Where to Buy:** Markets and shops in Cusco, Arequipa, Lima, and Puno.
  - **Price Range:** Varies based on the item.
  - **Website:** https://www.perufairtrade.com
- **Sustainable and Eco-Friendly Products:**
  - **Overview:** Many artisans in Peru are now using eco-friendly materials and sustainable practices to create their goods. Items made from recycled materials, organic dyes, or natural fibers are great options for eco-conscious travelers.
  - **Where to Buy:** Eco-friendly shops and fair-trade boutiques.
  - **Price Range:** $5-50 USD (S/ 20-200).
  - **Website:** https://www.sustainableperu.com

Chapter 11: Day Trips & Excursions

Peru is a land of diverse landscapes and rich history, and its day trips and excursions offer travelers the chance to explore some of the country's most stunning sites in a short amount of time. From the ancient ruins of the Sacred Valley to the arid desert of Ica, Peru provides a variety of unforgettable day experiences for every type of traveler. In this chapter, we highlight the best day trips and excursions, including pricing, locations, and booking details.

11.1 Sacred Valley Day Trips

Located just outside Cusco, the Sacred Valley is home to a wealth of ancient ruins, charming villages, and breathtaking landscapes. It's a perfect destination for a day trip that combines culture, history, and natural beauty.

- **Highlights:**
  - **Ollantaytambo:** Explore this impressive Inca site known for its terraces and ancient structures. It offers a great introduction to Inca architecture and history.
  - **Pisac:** Visit Pisac for its vibrant market and Inca ruins perched on the mountainside, offering panoramic views of the valley below.
  - **Moray:** Discover the unique circular terraces, thought to have been an agricultural laboratory used by the Incas.
  - **Maras Salt Mines:** These iconic salt pans are still used today and offer a scenic view into ancient salt extraction methods.
- **Best Time to Visit:** Year-round, though the dry season (May to September) is ideal for outdoor activities.
- **Pricing:**
  - **Private Tour:** Approx. $80-150 USD (S/ 280-500) per person.
  - **Group Tour:** Approx. $30-60 USD (S/ 100-200) per person.
- **Where to Book:**
  - https://www.cuscotravel.com
  - https://www.viator.com

11.2 Sacred Mountain of Ausangate

The Sacred Mountain of Ausangate, located in the southern Andes, is an awe-inspiring destination known for its towering snow-capped peaks, turquoise lakes, and vibrant landscapes. Though the trek is challenging, a day trip to the surrounding area offers unforgettable natural beauty.

- **Highlights:**
  - **Ausangate Trek:** This trek, typically lasting 4-5 days, takes you through rugged terrain with dramatic views of glaciers, high-altitude lakes, and remote villages. For those short on time, a day trip offers a taste of the surrounding areas.
  - **Rainbow Mountain (Vinicunca):** While not part of Ausangate itself, Rainbow Mountain is close by and is a popular day trip for its stunning colorful slopes.
- **Best Time to Visit:** May to October (dry season) for the best weather and trail conditions.
- **Pricing:**
  - **Day Trip to Rainbow Mountain:** Approx. $40-70 USD (S/ 140-250) per person.
  - **Ausangate Trek:** From $250-500 USD (S/ 900-1,800), depending on the tour and duration.
- **Where to Book:**
  - https://www.ausangateperu.com
  - https://www.rainbowmountainperu.com

11.3 The Inca Trail to Machu Picchu

One of the most iconic treks in the world, the Inca Trail takes you on a scenic journey through cloud forests and ancient Incan ruins, ultimately leading to the breathtaking Machu Picchu.

- **Highlights:**
  - **Stunning Scenery:** The Inca Trail offers breathtaking views of the Andes, lush forests, and the surrounding landscapes.

- **Historical Sites:** The trek includes stops at significant Inca ruins such as Wiñay Wayna, Inti Punku (Sun Gate), and the famous Dead Woman's Pass.
  - **Machu Picchu:** Completing the trail culminates in a sunrise arrival at Machu Picchu, where you can explore the ancient citadel.
- **Best Time to Visit:** April to October (dry season). The Inca Trail requires permits, which should be booked well in advance.
- **Pricing:**
  - **4-Day Trek:** Approx. $600-1,200 USD (S/ 2,200-4,500) per person, including permits, meals, and guide.
  - **Shorter Treks (e.g., 2-Day Inca Trail):** Approx. $300-700 USD (S/ 1,100-2,600) per person.
- **Where to Book:**
  - https://www.incatrailperu.com
  - https://www.viator.com

11.4 Day Trip to Colca Canyon & Arequipa

Colca Canyon, one of the deepest canyons in the world, is located just outside Arequipa. A day trip to this region offers awe-inspiring views, condor sightings, and opportunities to visit the local villages and hot springs.

- **Highlights:**
  - **Condor Watching:** Visit the Cruz del Condor viewpoint, where you can spot Andean condors soaring over the canyon.
  - **Thermal Springs:** After your hike, relax in the natural hot springs in Chivay for a soothing soak.
  - **Colca Valley Villages:** Explore picturesque villages like Yanque and Coporaque, where you can learn about traditional Andean life.
- **Best Time to Visit:** April to October (dry season) is ideal for visiting Colca Canyon.
- **Pricing:**
  - **Private Tour:** Approx. $80-150 USD (S/ 280-500) per person.
  - **Group Tour:** Approx. $40-70 USD (S/ 140-250) per person.
- **Where to Book:**

- https://www.arequipatravel.com
- https://www.viator.com

11.5 Ica & Huacachina: Desert Adventures

Ica and Huacachina provide a desert escape unlike any other, with activities like sandboarding, dune buggy rides, and opportunities to explore the desert's unique landscapes. Huacachina is a desert oasis that draws visitors for its natural beauty and adventurous offerings.

- **Highlights:**
  - **Huacachina Oasis:** A small oasis surrounded by towering sand dunes, perfect for relaxation and exploration.
  - **Sandboarding & Dune Buggy Rides:** Hop on a dune buggy for an adrenaline-filled ride across the desert, followed by a thrilling session of sandboarding.
  - **Ica Wine & Pisco Tasting:** Visit local vineyards to taste Peru's famous wines and pisco, and learn about the traditional methods of production.
- **Best Time to Visit:** March to November (dry season) offers the best conditions for desert activities.
- **Pricing:**
  - **Sandboarding & Dune Buggy Tour:** Approx. $30-50 USD (S/ 100-180) per person.
  - **Wine & Pisco Tasting Tour:** Approx. $20-40 USD (S/ 70-150) per person.
- **Where to Book:**
  - https://www.huacachinatours.com
  - https://www.icatelevision.com

Chapter 12: Health & Wellness

Traveling through Peru's varied terrain requires attention to your health, especially when venturing into the high-altitude regions like Cusco and Machu Picchu. This chapter provides practical advice for dealing with altitude sickness, healthcare options, wellness retreats, and staying active while exploring the country.

12.1 Managing Altitude Sickness

Altitude sickness, or acute mountain sickness (AMS), is a common issue for travelers visiting Peru's high-altitude destinations such as Cusco (3,400 meters) and Machu Picchu (2,430 meters). It occurs when the body struggles to adapt to lower oxygen levels at higher elevations.

Symptoms:

- Headaches
- Nausea
- Dizziness
- Shortness of breath
- Fatigue

Tips to Prevent and Address Altitude Sickness:

- **Gradual Acclimatization:** Spend a few days in lower altitude locations, like the Sacred Valley, before ascending to higher elevations. This allows your body to adjust.
- **Stay Hydrated:** Drink plenty of water and avoid alcohol or large meals that can exacerbate symptoms.
- **Medication:** Diamox (acetazolamide) can be used as a preventive treatment for altitude sickness. Be sure to consult with a healthcare provider before using it.
- **Rest:** On arrival at high altitudes, limit physical exertion until your body acclimates.
- **Coca Leaf Tea:** A traditional remedy, coca tea is commonly consumed to help with altitude-related symptoms.

Essential Advice:

If symptoms worsen, it's important to descend to a lower altitude. Seek medical assistance if necessary.

- **Medical Services:** There are clinics in places like **Cusco** (Hospital Regional de Cusco) and **Aguas Calientes** (nearest medical center to Machu Picchu) for emergency situations.

12.2 Healthcare & Pharmacies in Peru

While healthcare services are good in Peru's larger cities and popular tourist spots, healthcare in rural areas may be more limited. Knowing where to seek medical care is crucial during your travels.

Healthcare Facilities:

- **Cusco:** Reputable hospitals such as **Clinica Pardo** and **Clinica San Juan de Dios** provide solid healthcare options for visitors.
- **Lima: Clínica Anglo Americana** and **Clínica de la Mujer** offer excellent services, especially for travelers and expats.
- **Arequipa:** The **Hospital Regional Honorio Delgado** is a key healthcare provider in southern Peru.

Pharmacy Options:

Pharmacies are widely available in cities and towns. Chains like **Inkafarma** and **Farmacia Universitaria** offer general medications. For specific needs, it's advisable to carry any necessary prescription medications.

Emergency Contacts:

- **Ambulance:** 105
- **Police:** 105
- **Fire:** 116

Travel Insurance:

It's wise to invest in travel insurance that includes health coverage, especially one that covers medical evacuation, in case you are in remote areas where immediate care may not be accessible.

12.3 Wellness & Yoga Retreats

Peru is also known for its wellness offerings. From yoga retreats nestled in the Sacred Valley to spiritual experiences in the high Andes, travelers can easily incorporate relaxation and self-care into their journey.

Notable Wellness Retreats:

- **Sacred Valley: Willka T'ika** offers transformative yoga and wellness programs in a serene, eco-friendly environment surrounded by mountains.
    - **Location:** Urubamba, Sacred Valley
    - **Website:** http://www.willkatika.com
    - **Pricing:** Approx. $200-300 USD per night (includes meals and wellness sessions).
- **Machu Picchu:** For a wellness experience with a view of the lush jungle, **Inkaterra Machu Picchu Pueblo Hotel** provides wellness packages with spa services and yoga.
    - **Location:** Aguas Calientes
    - **Website:** https://www.inkaterra.com
    - **Pricing:** Approx. $350-500 USD per night.
- **Lake Titicaca: Posada del Inca** offers a unique blend of wellness and indigenous practices with yoga and spiritual healing on the shores of Lake Titicaca.
    - **Location:** Puno
    - **Website:** https://www.posadadelinca.com
    - **Pricing:** Approx. $150-200 USD per night.

Retreat Features:

- Yoga, meditation, and mindfulness practices
- Organic, healthy meals with a focus on Peruvian ingredients
- Detox programs and spa treatments

12.4 Peruvian Herbal Medicine

Peruvian traditional medicine, based on a wide variety of native plants, is still commonly practiced. Many visitors turn to herbal remedies to address common ailments such as headaches, fatigue, and digestive issues.

Popular Peruvian Herbs and Remedies:

- **Coca Leaves:** Traditionally used to treat altitude sickness, these leaves are chewed or brewed into tea.
- **Ayahuasca:** A powerful hallucinogenic brew used in shamanic ceremonies for spiritual healing.
- **Maca Root:** Known for its energy-boosting properties, maca is often consumed in powder form and added to smoothies or teas.
- **Chanca Piedra:** This herb is believed to help dissolve kidney stones and treat liver conditions.
- **Cat's Claw:** Used for its anti-inflammatory properties, cat's claw is believed to enhance immune function.

Where to Find Herbal Remedies:

- **Local Markets:** In Cusco's **San Pedro Market** or Lima's **Mercado de Flores**, you can purchase herbal teas and remedies.
- **Healing Centers:** Shamanic healing practices using plants like ayahuasca are offered by various spiritual centers in the Sacred Valley.

12.5 Staying Active: Peru's Outdoor Sports

Peru's diverse landscape offers endless opportunities for outdoor sports and activities, making it a perfect destination for active travelers.

Popular Outdoor Activities:

- **Trekking:** The iconic Inca Trail to Machu Picchu is the most popular trek, but there are also alternative routes like the **Salkantay** and **Lares Treks**. The **Ausangate Trek** offers a remote, breathtaking alternative.
  - **Locations:** Sacred Valley, Colca Canyon, and the Inca Trail.

- **Pricing:** Guided tours typically cost between $40-150 USD per day.
- **Mountain Biking:** The Sacred Valley and Cusco region offer excellent mountain biking opportunities, with trails for all skill levels.
  - **Locations:** Sacred Valley, Ollantaytambo, Pisac.
  - **Pricing:** Rentals typically range from $30-70 USD per day.
- **Surfing:** Peru's Pacific coast is home to world-class surf, particularly in regions like **Máncora**, **Lima**, and **Punta Hermosa**. Whether you're a beginner or an expert, there's something for everyone.
  - **Locations:** Máncora, Punta Hermosa, and Lobitos.
  - **Pricing:** Surfboard rentals are typically around $10-20 USD per day, while lessons cost $40-70 USD per session.
- **Paragliding:** The stunning landscapes of Peru, including the **Sacred Valley** and **Lima**, offer great opportunities for paragliding.
  - **Locations:** Miraflores (Lima), Sacred Valley.
  - **Pricing:** Tandem flights typically cost around $80-150 USD.

Chapter 13: Shopping & Souvenirs

Peru offers a wide range of vibrant markets and artisan shops where visitors can purchase everything from unique souvenirs to locally crafted textiles and jewelry. Shopping here provides an excellent opportunity to connect with the country's rich culture and history. This chapter covers the best places to shop, highlights authentic Peruvian crafts, and offers advice on making ethical purchasing choices.

13.1 Traditional Markets

Peruvian markets are bustling hubs where locals and tourists alike can shop for everything from fresh produce to handmade goods. These markets are perfect for those seeking unique souvenirs or simply wanting to experience the vibrant culture of Peru.

Top Markets to Explore:

- **San Pedro Market (Cusco):** This famous market is a must-visit for those in Cusco, offering a vast selection of local produce, spices, and artisanal crafts. You'll find colorful textiles, pottery, jewelry, and small gifts.
  - **Location:** Cusco, Av. Pardo y 2 de Mayo
  - **Highlights:** Traditional Andean food items like **maíz morado** (purple corn) and **coca leaves**, plus woven textiles and pottery.
  - **Website:** http://www.cuscoturismo.com
- **Mercado de las Brujas (Lima):** Known as the "Witches' Market," this spot is ideal for those interested in spiritual items like herbs and potions, as well as indigenous handicrafts.
  - **Location:** Lima, Jr. Camaná, Centro Histórico
  - **Highlights: Pachamama** figurines, incense, and colorful Andean masks.
  - **Website:** https://www.peru.travel
- **Pisac Market (Sacred Valley):** A famous market known for its vibrant local crafts, particularly woven textiles and silver jewelry. The scenic views of the Sacred Valley make shopping here an even more enjoyable experience.
  - **Location:** Pisac, Sacred Valley

- Highlights: Handmade **ceramics**, **alpaca wool** garments, and **silver jewelry**.
  - Website: http://www.pisacmarket.com
- **Manuel A. Odría Market (Arequipa):** This local market is less touristy and offers a great selection of fresh foods, spices, and handcrafted textiles and goods.
  - **Location:** Arequipa, Av. Odría
  - **Highlights:** Local cheeses, **cactus fruit**, and **traditional woolen goods**.

Pricing Range:

- Small souvenirs: $1–10 USD
- Handcrafted textiles: $15–50 USD
- Jewelry: $10–50 USD

13.2 Unique Gifts & Artisan Crafts

Peru is home to a variety of traditional crafts, and shopping for artisan goods here is a perfect way to bring home a piece of the country's cultural heritage.

Top Artisan Gifts:

- **Jewelry:** Peruvian silver jewelry is renowned for its craftsmanship and often incorporates beautiful natural stones like **lapis lazuli**, **turquoise**, and **quartz**. You'll find a range of pieces from earrings to rings and necklaces.
  - **Where to Buy: Ollantaytambo, Pisac, Cusco**
  - **Price:** $10–100 USD depending on craftsmanship.
- **Textiles:** Peru is famous for its **alpaca wool** and **cotton** textiles. These can range from scarves and blankets to ponchos and shawls, all handwoven using traditional techniques.
  - **Where to Buy: Sacred Valley, Arequipa, Cusco**
  - **Price:** $15–60 USD for scarves, $40–150 USD for ponchos or blankets.
- **Ceramics & Pottery:** Traditional **Peruvian ceramics** often feature intricate, hand-painted designs inspired by ancient **Nazca** and **Inca** motifs, making them a unique souvenir or home decor piece.
  - **Where to Buy: Chinchero** (Sacred Valley), **Nazca**

- **Price:** $10–50 USD depending on the piece.
- **Retablos:** Colorful wooden boxes, often depicting Andean life or religious figures, these hand-painted items are iconic in Peru and make for a striking gift or memento.
  - **Where to Buy: Ayacucho, Cusco**
  - **Price:** $20–60 USD

13.3 Where to Buy Peruvian Textiles

Peruvian textiles are widely recognized for their craftsmanship, with **alpaca wool** being one of the most sought-after materials. Many of these textiles are made using ancient weaving techniques that have been passed down through generations.

Top Places for Textile Shopping:

- **Sacred Valley (Chinchero, Pisac):** These towns are known for their high-quality, handwoven textiles, especially those made from **alpaca wool**. You can find everything from scarves to blankets and ponchos.
  - **Where to Buy:** Local weaving cooperatives in **Chinchero** and **Pisac**.
  - **Price:** $30–150 USD for scarves, $50–200 USD for ponchos or blankets.
- **Arequipa:** A well-known center for **alpaca wool**, Arequipa offers some of the finest and softest textiles in the country, from clothing to home decor.
  - **Where to Buy: Arequipa's artisan markets** or specialty stores.
  - **Price:** $40–150 USD for sweaters, scarves, and ponchos.
- **Cusco:** The **Centro de Textiles Tradicionales** in Cusco is a wonderful place to purchase authentic textiles, where you can learn about the weaving process and buy certified handmade garments.
  - **Where to Buy: Centro de Textiles Tradicionales** (Cusco)
  - **Website:** http://www.textilescusco.org
  - **Price:** $20–60 USD for scarves, up to $150 USD for larger items like blankets.

13.4 Ethical Shopping Tips

Shopping ethically in Peru ensures that the local artisans are fairly compensated and that your purchases are responsibly made. Here are some tips to help you shop with care:

1. Choose Fair Trade Products:
Fair trade organizations like **Manos del Peru** work closely with indigenous artisans to guarantee fair wages and support local communities.

2. Shop from Cooperatives:
Supporting local cooperatives or purchasing directly from artisans helps to ensure that the money stays within the community. Many communities rely on their crafts as a primary source of income.

3. Look for Eco-Friendly Products:
Many Peruvian artisans are embracing sustainable practices by using **organic cotton**, natural dyes, and eco-friendly materials like **recycled wool** or **eco-friendly alpaca fibers**.

4. Avoid Mass-Produced Souvenirs:
Opt for handmade, locally crafted items rather than mass-produced souvenirs that do not reflect the region's authentic culture and craftsmanship.

5. Be Conscious of Animal Products:
While **alpaca wool** is a sought-after material, always inquire about its sourcing to ensure that it is ethically obtained. Choose products that support responsible and humane practices.

Ethical Shopping Resources:

- **Manos del Peru:** A Fair Trade organization that connects artisans across Peru with ethical buyers.
  - **Website:** http://www.manosdelperu.com
- **Peruvian Connection:** A Fair Trade company that sells traditional Peruvian textiles and apparel, working directly with local artisans.
  - **Website:** https://www.peruvianconnection.com

Price Range for Ethical Products:

- Handwoven textiles: $20–100 USD
- Jewelry and crafts: $10–60 USD

Chapter 14: Safety & Security

Peru is a popular destination for travelers seeking adventure, culture, and history, but like any travel experience, it's important to be aware of safety and security considerations. This chapter provides essential information on staying safe while traveling, understanding local laws, and knowing what to do in case of emergencies. With a few precautionary measures, you can enjoy Peru's beauty with confidence.

14.1 Crime & Safety Precautions

While Peru is a generally safe country to visit, like any popular tourist destination, it has areas where petty crime—such as pickpocketing and theft—can occur. Understanding common safety risks and taking preventive steps will help ensure a smooth and enjoyable trip.

Common Safety Concerns:

- **Pickpocketing & Theft:** In crowded areas like markets, bus stations, or tourist sites (e.g., **Machu Picchu**, **Plaza de Armas** in Cusco), petty theft can occur. Always be aware of your surroundings and keep your valuables secure.
  - **Tips:**
    - Use anti-theft backpacks or money belts.
    - Avoid carrying large amounts of cash.
    - Never leave your bags unattended, even in restaurants or cafes.
- **Street Scams:** Some tourists fall victim to street scams, such as fake petitions or offers for "free" items that later demand money. Be cautious when approached by strangers, especially in busy tourist areas.
  - **Tips:**
    - Politely decline offers for unsolicited help or services.
    - Avoid engaging in unsolicited exchanges, especially when walking around at night.
- **Taxi Safety:** While taxis are common in Lima and other cities, it's recommended to use **registered taxis** or rideshare apps (like **Uber**, **Beat**, or **Cabify**) for more security.
  - **Tips:**

- Use rideshare apps rather than hailing taxis from the street.
- If using a taxi, ensure the driver is licensed and the meter is on.
- Always agree on a fare beforehand if using a non-metered taxi.
- **Avoiding Isolated Areas at Night:** Certain areas in major cities such as **Lima** and **Cusco** are best avoided after dark. Stick to well-lit, populated streets and avoid walking through alleyways or unfamiliar neighborhoods.
  - **Safety Areas:** Tourist districts like **Miraflores** (Lima) and **San Blas** (Cusco) are generally safer, but always stay vigilant.

14.2 Emergency Contacts & Services

Knowing where to go and who to contact in case of an emergency can make a big difference during your trip. Here are key emergency contacts and services to have on hand:

Emergency Numbers:

- **Police:** 105
- **Ambulance:** 106
- **Fire Department:** 117
- **Tourist Police (POLTUR):** 513-5100 (Lima)
  - These officers are trained to assist foreign visitors and can be a helpful resource in case of theft or emergencies.

Hospitals & Clinics:

- **Clínica Internacional (Lima):**
  - **Address:** Av. Pardo y Aliaga 640, San Isidro, Lima
  - **Phone:** +51 1 611-8000
  - Known for its high-quality medical care for foreigners.
- **Clinica de Salud, Cusco:**
  - **Address:** Av. Tullumayo 528, Cusco
  - **Phone:** +51 84 232-088
  - Offers medical services for tourists and locals alike.

Consular Services:

- **U.S. Embassy (Lima):**
  - **Address:** Av. Pardo y 2 de Mayo 600, San Isidro, Lima
  - **Phone:** +51 1 618-2000
  - Provides emergency assistance for U.S. citizens, including lost passports or legal assistance.
- **UK Embassy (Lima):**
  - **Address:** Av. Pardo y 2 de Mayo 215, San Isidro, Lima
  - **Phone:** +51 1 617-3000
  - Offers consular support for British nationals.

14.3 Health & Travel Insurance

Health risks in Peru can be mitigated with proper precautions, but having travel insurance is highly recommended. Travel insurance helps cover unexpected medical costs, cancellations, and lost baggage.

Travel Health Recommendations:

- **Altitude Sickness:** If traveling to high-altitude areas like **Cusco**, **Machu Picchu**, or **Arequipa**, be aware of the potential for altitude sickness, especially if you're coming from a low-altitude location. Symptoms include dizziness, headaches, and nausea.
  - **Prevention Tips:**
    - Acclimatize by spending a few days in Cusco before heading to higher altitudes.
    - Stay hydrated and avoid alcohol in the first few days.
    - Take medications (like **Diamox**) if recommended by your doctor.
- **Vaccinations:** Travelers should be up to date on routine vaccines (MMR, diphtheria, etc.) and consider vaccines for **hepatitis A**, **hepatitis B**, **typhoid**, and **yellow fever**, especially if visiting the **Amazon** region.
  - Consult a healthcare provider before traveling for personalized vaccination advice.
- **Travel Insurance:** Comprehensive travel insurance is crucial, covering medical expenses, cancellations, and lost baggage. Look for insurance that includes emergency evacuation and coverage for activities like trekking or adventure sports.

14.4 Avoiding Scams

While Peru is generally safe, scams targeting tourists can still occur. Here are some common scams and how to avoid them:

- **Overcharging in Taxis:** Some taxi drivers may attempt to overcharge tourists, especially if they do not use a meter.
  - **Tip:** Always confirm the price in advance or opt for rideshare services.
- **Fake Tour Operators:** Unofficial tour operators may promise great deals but provide substandard services.
  - **Tip:** Always book tours through reputable companies or your hotel. Look for **TripAdvisor** reviews or recommendations from trusted sources.
- **ATM Skimming:** Be cautious when using ATMs, especially in tourist-heavy areas, as scams such as ATM skimming can happen.
  - **Tip:** Use ATMs in reputable locations like banks, and cover the keypad when entering your PIN.
- **Petition and Charity Scams:** In some areas, you may encounter individuals asking for donations or signatures for fake causes. Always be wary of unsolicited requests.
  - **Tip:** Politely decline and walk away.

14.5 Local Laws & Customs

Understanding and respecting local laws and customs is essential for a smooth and enjoyable visit. Here are some important things to know before traveling in Peru:

Legal Considerations:

- **Drugs:** The possession and trafficking of illegal drugs are serious crimes in Peru, with severe penalties, including long prison sentences.
  - **Tip:** Do not attempt to buy, sell, or use illegal substances in Peru.

- **Alcohol Consumption:** The legal drinking age in Peru is 18 years old. Public drinking is generally acceptable, but excessive drinking and disorderly behavior can lead to fines or arrest.
  - **Tip:** Drink responsibly, especially in rural or unfamiliar areas.
- **Photography Restrictions:** Some religious sites, indigenous communities, and government buildings may prohibit photography. Always ask before taking photos to avoid offending locals or breaking the law.
  - **Tip:** Respect "no photography" signs and ask locals for permission before taking their photo.

Cultural Etiquette:

- **Greetings:** A handshake is the most common form of greeting. In more informal settings, a kiss on the cheek may be exchanged between friends or family.
  - **Tip:** If meeting someone for the first time, a handshake is appropriate.
- **Punctuality:** Peruvians value punctuality for formal events, but being slightly late is often acceptable in social settings.
  - **Tip:** Be mindful of time, especially for business meetings or tours.

Chapter 15: Sustainable Travel

As global awareness about the environmental impact of tourism grows, travelers are increasingly seeking ways to reduce their footprint. Peru, with its rich biodiversity and cultural heritage, offers unique opportunities for sustainable tourism. This chapter outlines how you can explore Peru responsibly, supporting local communities and preserving the country's natural beauty.

15.1 Eco-Friendly Travel in Peru

Peru is home to a diverse range of ecosystems, from the **Amazon Rainforest** to the towering **Andes Mountains**, making sustainable travel practices especially important. There are several ways to lessen your environmental impact while enjoying all that this magnificent country has to offer.

Eco-Friendly Travel Tips:

- **Minimize Plastic Use:** Peru struggles with plastic waste, particularly in remote regions. Bring a reusable water bottle, avoid single-use plastic bags, and look for businesses that prioritize sustainable packaging.
  - **Recommendation:** A **water filter bottle** like **GRAYL** is an eco-friendly way to stay hydrated without contributing to plastic waste.
- **Eco-Conscious Accommodation:** Many eco-lodges and hotels in Peru focus on sustainability through practices like waste reduction, water conservation, and renewable energy. Look for certifications such as **Green Globe** or **EarthCheck** for environmentally responsible properties.
  - **Example: Inkaterra Machu Picchu Pueblo Hotel** in the **Sacred Valley** is an eco-lodge that promotes conservation and offers nature-based activities.
  - **Website:** https://www.inkaterra.com
  - **Price Range:** $250+ per night.
- **Sustainable Tours:** Opt for tour companies that prioritize eco-friendly travel. Many in **Cusco** and **Arequipa** now offer carbon-neutral tours and educational experiences focused on conservation.

- Example: **Explorandes** offers eco-conscious treks in the Andes, including the **Salkantay Trek**.
- Website: https://www.explorandes.com

15.2 Community-Based Tourism

A fantastic way to experience Peru's culture while supporting sustainable development is through **community-based tourism (CBT)**. CBT allows travelers to immerse themselves in local traditions while directly benefiting indigenous communities.

Opportunities for Community Tourism:

- **Sacred Valley Homestays:** Stay with local families in **Chinchero** or **Ollantaytambo** to experience Andean culture first-hand. These homestays offer activities like weaving workshops and farm-to-table meals.
  - **Cost:** Approximately $30–$50 per night.
  - **Highlights:** Learn about local agriculture, participate in cooking classes, and discover indigenous handicrafts.
- **Amazon Community Experiences:** In the **Amazon**, eco-lodges in places like **Iquitos** and **Puerto Maldonado** offer immersive stays with local tribes, where you can learn about sustainable farming practices and conservation efforts.
  - **Example: Napo Wildlife Center** is run by the **Anangu** community in the Amazon, where you can stay in eco-friendly cabins and join wildlife tours.
  - Website: https://www.napowildlifecenter.com
  - **Price:** $200 per night, full board.

15.3 Protecting Peru's Natural Wonders

Peru's iconic landscapes, from **Machu Picchu** to the **Colca Canyon**, are natural treasures that require care and protection. As a visitor, there are many ways to contribute to the conservation of these sites.

How to Protect Peru's Natural Wonders:

- **Adhere to Conservation Rules:** Peru has strict regulations to protect its natural sites. Always stay on marked paths, avoid disturbing wildlife, and follow park guidelines.
  - **Tip:** Tickets for **Machu Picchu** must be purchased in advance, and visitor numbers are regulated to help preserve the site. Ticket prices range from $45 to $75 depending on the tour type.
  - **Website:** machupicchu.gob.pe
- **Support Wildlife Protection Efforts:** Participate in wildlife conservation tours or donate to organizations working to protect Peru's endangered species. **The Amazon Conservation Association** offers educational tours in the **Madre de Dios** region.
  - **Website:** https://www.amazonconservation.org
  - **Price:** Day tours from $50 per person.
- **Engage in Reforestation:** Volunteer or join reforestation projects in the Amazon or the Andes, where you can help restore native forests and support conservation initiatives.
  - **Example: Rainforest Expeditions** offers eco-tours that include reforestation efforts and sustainable farming activities.
  - **Website:** https://www.rainforestexpeditions.com

15.4 Supporting Sustainable Local Businesses

Supporting businesses that prioritize sustainability and fair trade practices helps drive the local economy and ensures that the benefits of tourism are shared equitably.

How to Support Sustainable Businesses:

- **Buy Fair-Trade Goods:** Shop for authentic Peruvian handicrafts in local markets like **San Blas** in **Cusco** or **Pisac Market** in the Sacred Valley. Look for goods made with eco-friendly materials such as **alpaca wool** or **tagua nut**.
  - **Tip:** Purchasing directly from artisans ensures they are fairly compensated and encourages responsible production.
- **Dine at Eco-Conscious Restaurants:** Support restaurants that use local, organic ingredients and adopt environmentally-friendly practices. For

example, **Café de la Paz** in **Cusco** focuses on organic ingredients and supports local farmers.
- o **Website:** https://www.cafedelpazcusco.com
- o **Price:** Average meal cost $10–$20.
- **Stay in Eco-Friendly Lodging:** Choose accommodations that prioritize sustainability through energy efficiency and waste reduction. The **Sacred Valley** offers many eco-lodges that promote responsible tourism.
  - o **Example: Sumaq Machu Picchu Hotel** is an environmentally-conscious hotel that emphasizes local culture, conservation, and sustainability.
  - o **Website:** https://www.sumaqhotelperu.com

15.5 Travel Tips for Minimizing Environmental Impact

Here are some practical suggestions to help you minimize your environmental impact while traveling in Peru:

- **Use Public Transport:** To reduce your carbon footprint, rely on public transportation such as the **Metropolitano Bus** in **Lima** or shared rides with services like **Uber** or **Beat**.
  - o **Tip:** The **Metropolitano Bus** is a fast and affordable way to travel around **Lima**, with a fare of around $0.50 per ride.
- **Pack Light & Avoid Waste:** Bring reusable bags, refillable water bottles, and avoid disposable products to minimize waste. Choose biodegradable toiletries like soap bars or shampoo bars over plastic bottled products.
- **Conserve Water and Energy:** Peru faces water shortages, so conserve water by taking shorter showers, reusing towels, and turning off lights and electronics when not in use.
- **Support Conservation Projects:** Consider donating to or volunteering with organizations working to preserve Peru's ecosystems and indigenous cultures. Your contribution can directly impact local communities and conservation efforts.

Chapter 16: Peru's History & Culture

Peru is a country rich in history, shaped by ancient civilizations, colonial rule, and a vibrant indigenous heritage. In this chapter, we explore the profound impact of the **Inca Empire**, the lasting influence of Spanish colonization, and the ongoing traditions of indigenous communities that form the backbone of modern Peru.

16.1 The Incas: Peru's Ancient Civilization

The **Inca Empire**, one of the largest pre-Columbian empires in the Americas, dominated the Andean region from the early 1400s until the Spanish conquest in 1532. Known for their impressive architecture, engineering feats, and agricultural innovations, the Incas left behind a rich cultural legacy that still resonates in Peru today.

Inca Highlights:

- **Machu Picchu:** This iconic Incan citadel, perched high in the Andes, remains one of the most significant archaeological sites in the world, attracting millions of visitors each year.
  - **Location: Machu Picchu**, Sacred Valley.
- **Incan Roads & Architecture:** The Incas built an extensive network of roads that connected vast parts of their empire. The **Qhapaq Ñan**, or Inca Trail, is still used by hikers today. The remains of **Sacsayhuamán**, near Cusco, demonstrate their advanced stonework.
- **Religious Practices:** The Incas revered **Inti**, the Sun God, and celebrated various festivals to honor their deities. They also worshipped **Pachamama**, the Earth Mother, whose influence is still felt in many indigenous communities.

Inca Contributions:

- **Agriculture:** The Incas mastered the art of farming in the challenging Andean terrain, creating terraces and sophisticated irrigation systems that allowed them to grow crops in high-altitude areas.

- **Textiles:** The Incas produced intricate textiles from **alpaca wool** and cotton, and this tradition is still alive in rural Andean villages.

16.2 Colonial Legacy: Spanish Influence on Peru

In 1532, **Francisco Pizarro** and his conquistadors arrived in Peru, beginning nearly 300 years of Spanish colonial rule. The Spanish introduced Catholicism, their language, and a new social order that reshaped Peruvian society.

Colonial Influences:

- **Catholicism:** The Spanish brought Catholicism to Peru, and churches, monasteries, and cathedrals were built across the country. Examples include the **Cathedral of Lima** and **Church of San Francisco**.
    - **Location: Plaza de Armas, Lima.**
    - **Admission:** Approx. $3–$5.
- **Colonial Architecture:** Spanish architectural styles, including baroque churches and colonial plazas, still dominate the cities of **Lima**, **Arequipa**, and **Cusco**. Many of these buildings are now UNESCO World Heritage sites.
- **Social Hierarchy:** The Spanish established a rigid caste system, with Spanish settlers at the top, followed by mixed-race mestizos, indigenous people, and enslaved Africans. This social structure continues to influence modern Peruvian society.
- **Language:** While the Spanish language became dominant, **Quechua** and **Aymara** continue to be spoken by millions of Peruvians, particularly in rural regions.

16.3 Indigenous Communities: Languages & Traditions

Despite the impact of Spanish colonization, Peru's indigenous communities have preserved their languages, traditions, and cultures for centuries. Groups such as the **Quechua, Aymara**, and **Amazonian tribes** continue to play an integral role in Peruvian society.

Indigenous Languages & Tribes:

- **Quechua:** Spoken by millions, **Quechua** was the language of the Incas and remains the second most spoken language in Peru after Spanish.
- **Aymara:** The **Aymara** people, who live near **Lake Titicaca**, have a distinct language and culture. Aymara is also spoken in parts of **Bolivia** and **Chile**.
- **Amazonian Tribes:** In the vast **Amazon Rainforest**, tribes like the **Asháninka, Shipibo**, and **Yagua** maintain traditional lifestyles and rely on the forest for their sustenance and spiritual practices.

Indigenous Festivals:

- **Inti Raymi:** This Inca festival celebrating the **Sun God** Inti takes place every year in **Cusco** and is a spectacular display of ancient rituals, music, and dance.
  - **Date:** June 24.
  - **Location: Sacsayhuamán, Cusco.**
  - **Tickets:** Around $10–$30.
- **Carnival of the Andes:** In towns like **Tingobamba**, locals celebrate with vibrant dances, costumes, and festivities that reflect Andean traditions.

16.4 Peru's Role in Modern South America

Peru is a key player in South America, known for its rich cultural heritage, economic growth, and international influence. While it faces ongoing challenges such as poverty and environmental concerns, Peru is also at the forefront of preserving its heritage while navigating the modern world.

Modern Contributions:

- **Economic Development:** Peru has seen significant economic growth in recent years, primarily driven by its mining, agriculture, and tourism sectors. It is a major global producer of minerals like **copper**, **silver**, and **gold**.
- **Cultural Renaissance:** Traditional Peruvian arts are experiencing a revival, particularly in **gastronomy**. World-renowned chefs such as **Gastón Acurio** have put **Lima** on the culinary map. **Andean music** and **indigenous crafts** are also gaining global recognition.
- **Political Influence:** Peru plays an active role in regional affairs, participating in groups like the **Andean Community** and the **Pacific Alliance**. It also champions environmental protection, particularly in the **Amazon**.

Challenges in Modern Peru:

- **Environmental Issues:** Peru's rapid development has led to environmental challenges, such as deforestation and pollution from mining and oil extraction. Efforts are underway to balance economic growth with conservation.
- **Indigenous Rights:** Land rights for indigenous groups, especially in the Amazon, remain a contentious issue. The push for greater protection of indigenous lands is an ongoing struggle.
- **Tourism:** While tourism contributes significantly to the economy, it also poses challenges in terms of sustainability. The preservation of cultural and natural resources requires careful management to ensure that tourism benefits both local communities and the environment.

Chapter 17: Language Guide

Peru is a bilingual country with **Spanish** as the official language and **Quechua** (along with **Aymara**) spoken by many indigenous communities, particularly in the highlands and rural regions. Understanding some basic phrases in both languages will enhance your travel experience, allowing you to connect more meaningfully with locals. In this chapter, we provide essential phrases in **Spanish** and **Quechua**, key greetings, polite expressions, and pronunciation tips to help you navigate Peru more confidently.

17.1 Spanish Phrases for Travelers

While **Spanish** is widely spoken throughout Peru, certain regional accents and expressions may vary. Here are some key phrases for travelers to use in everyday situations:

Greetings & Polite Phrases:

- **Hello / Hi:** *Hola*
- **Good morning:** *Buenos días*
- **Good afternoon:** *Buenas tardes*
- **Good evening / Good night:** *Buenas noches*
- **How are you?:** *¿Cómo estás?*
- **I'm fine, thank you:** *Estoy bien, gracias*
- **Nice to meet you:** *Mucho gusto*
- **Please:** *Por favor*
- **Thank you:** *Gracias*
- **You're welcome:** *De nada*
- **Excuse me:** *Disculpe / Perdón*
- **Goodbye:** *Adiós*

Useful Travel Phrases:

- **Where is...?** *¿Dónde está...?*
- **How much is it?** *¿Cuánto cuesta?*
- **I don't understand:** *No entiendo*

- **Do you speak English?** *¿Habla inglés?*
- **I'm lost:** *Estoy perdido/a*
- **Can you help me?:** *¿Puede ayudarme?*
- **What time is it?:** *¿Qué hora es?*
- **Bathroom:** *Baño*
- **Water:** *Agua*
- **I need a doctor:** *Necesito un médico*
- **Emergency:** *Emergencia*

Numbers (1-10):

- 1 - *Uno*
- 2 - *Dos*
- 3 - *Tres*
- 4 - *Cuatro*
- 5 - *Cinco*
- 6 - *Seis*
- 7 - *Siete*
- 8 - *Ocho*
- 9 - *Nueve*
- 10 - *Diez*

17.2 Key Quechua Words & Phrases

Quechua is one of the oldest languages in the world, and it remains a significant part of Peruvian culture, especially in rural areas of the **Andes**. While Spanish is more commonly used in urban areas, knowing a few Quechua phrases will endear you to local people and show respect for their traditions.

Greetings & Polite Phrases:

- **Hello / Hi:** *Ñuqanchik kachkan*
- **Good morning:** *Allimpa p'unchay*
- **Good evening:** *Allimpa ch'isi*
- **How are you?:** *Imaynalla kachkanki?*
- **I'm fine, thank you:** *Ñuqaqa alli kachkani, sipaski*

- **Thank you:** *Sulpayki*
- **Goodbye:** *Tupananchiskama* (Until we meet again)
- **Please:** *Ama hina*
- **Excuse me:** *Ñuqaqa kamachiy*

Basic Questions:

- **Where is...?** *Maypi...?*
- **How much is it?** *Kunanmi huk k'anchay?*
- **What is your name?:** *Ima sutiyki?*
- **My name is...** *Ñuqaqa... sutiyki*
- **I don't understand:** *Manan alliymi*
- **Can you help me?:** *Ñuqaqa munanki?*
- **Water:** *Waqi*
- **Food:** *Mikhuy*
- **Where are you from?:** *Maypi kanki?*
- **I am from...** *Ñuqaqa... rimayku*

17.3 Common Greetings & Polite Expressions

Spanish Greetings:

- **¡Hola!** (Hello!)
- **¡Buenos días!** (Good morning!)
- **¡Buenas tardes!** (Good afternoon!)
- **¡Buenas noches!** (Good night!)
- **¿Cómo estás?** (How are you?)
- **¿Qué tal?** (What's up?)
- **¿Cómo te va?** (How's it going?)
- **Mucho gusto** (Nice to meet you)
- **¿Qué pasa?** (What's happening?)
- **¿Todo bien?** (Is everything good?)

Quechua Greetings:

- **Ñuqanchik kachkan** (Hello, we are fine)
- **Allimpa p'unchay** (Good morning)

- **Imaynalla kachkanki?** (How are you?)
- **Sumaq kawsay** (Beautiful life)
- **Ñuqaqa alli kachkani** (I am fine)
- **Tupananchiskama** (Goodbye, until we meet again)

Polite Expressions (Spanish & Quechua):

- **Por favor** (Please)
- **Gracias** (Thank you)
- **Disculpe** (Excuse me)
- **Perdón** (Sorry)
- **De nada** (You're welcome)
- **Sí, por supuesto** (Yes, of course)
- **No hay problema** (No problem)
- **Lo siento** (I'm sorry)
- **Todo bien** (It's all good)

17.4 Pronunciation Tips

Spanish Pronunciation:

- **Vowels:**
  - A sounds like "ah"
  - E sounds like "eh"
  - I sounds like "ee"
  - O sounds like "oh"
  - U sounds like "oo"
- **Consonants:**
  - The letter **"h"** is silent (e.g., *hola* – "hello").
  - The letter **"v"** sounds like **"b"** (e.g., *viento* – "wind" sounds like *biento*).
  - The letter **"ll"** is pronounced like "y" in *yes* (e.g., *llama* – "flame" sounds like *yama*).
  - The letter **"j"** is pronounced like an English **"h"** (e.g., *jugar* – "to play").

Quechua Pronunciation:

- **Vowels:** Quechua vowels are similar to Spanish vowels:

- A sounds like "ah"
- I sounds like "ee"
- U sounds like "oo"
- **Consonants:**
  - The **"ch"** sound is pronounced as in "chocolate" (e.g., *chaska* – "star").
  - The **"q"** is a harder sound, almost like "k" but pronounced deeper in the throat (e.g., *qori* – "gold").

Common Challenges:

- The letter **"r"** in Spanish is rolled or trilled, so practicing this sound can be helpful when speaking.
- **Quechua** has many glottal sounds, so pay attention to the subtle difference in sounds like **"k"** and **"q."**

Chapter 18: Practical Travel Tips

Exploring Peru is a thrilling adventure, but preparing for your trip is essential to ensure a smooth and enjoyable experience. This chapter will guide you through the practical aspects of managing time and money, navigating transportation, avoiding common travel pitfalls, packing for the diverse environments, and keeping your belongings safe while traveling.

18.1 Managing Time & Currency

Time Zone:

- Peru operates on **Peru Time (UTC-5)**, the same as Eastern Standard Time (EST) during daylight saving time in the U.S. Peru does not observe daylight savings, so time differences may vary depending on the season.

Currency:

- The official currency is **Sol (PEN)**.
- **Currency Exchange:** Foreign currencies, including **USD**, are often accepted, but exchange rates can vary. It's advisable to check rates before exchanging at banks, ATMs, or currency exchange offices.
  - *Exchange Rate (2024):* 1 USD ≈ 3.70 PEN (subject to change).
  - **ATMs:** Available in most urban areas, though remote regions may have limited access. Be aware of foreign transaction fees from your bank.
- **Cash vs. Cards:** Credit and debit cards are widely accepted in cities, but rural areas and markets often prefer cash. Carry enough **S/** (Soles) for small purchases, local transport, and tips.

Budgeting & Costs:

- Peru is affordable for most travelers, but prices vary by region and tourism level.
  - **Mid-range accommodation**: S/ 150–S/ 350 per night.
  - **Street food**: S/ 5–S/ 15 for a snack or light meal.
  - **Restaurant meals**: S/ 30–S/ 70 per person.

- **Attractions**: Entrance fees for major sites like Machu Picchu range from **S/ 50–S/ 100**.

Tipping:

- Tipping is appreciated but not mandatory. In restaurants, a 10% tip is common if not already included. For guides or drivers, tips can range from S/ 10–S/ 50, depending on service.

18.2 Navigating Peru's Transportation System

Public Transportation in Major Cities:

- **Lima's Metro:** The **Lima Metro**, especially **Line 1**, offers a quick and affordable way to travel across the city, with fares around **S/ 1.50**.
- **Buses & Microbuses:** These are a cheap and popular option for getting around, but be prepared for crowded conditions.
- **Taxis & Rideshares:** While taxis are common, **Uber** and **Cabify** are safer alternatives for getting around Lima and other cities. Fares typically start around **S/ 5**.

Intercity Travel:

- **Domestic Flights:** Peru has several domestic airlines, including **LATAM** and **Avianca**, offering flights between major cities like Lima, Cusco, and Arequipa. Prices range from **S/ 100–S/ 500** depending on the route and timing.
- **Long-distance Buses:** Bus travel is economical, with companies like **Cruz del Sur** and **PeruBus** offering comfortable, overnight services.
  - Example fares:
    - Lima to Cusco: **S/ 100–S/ 250** (21-hour ride)
    - Lima to Arequipa: **S/ 80–S/ 150** (16-hour ride)
- **Trains:** **PeruRail** and **IncaRail** operate scenic trains to **Machu Picchu**, with one-way tickets ranging from **USD 70–USD 300**.

Taxis in Smaller Cities:

- In smaller towns, taxis may not have meters, so it's essential to negotiate the price upfront. Short trips typically cost **S/ 5–S/ 15**.

18.3 Common Travel Mistakes to Avoid

1. Underestimating Time at Attractions:

- Popular sites like **Machu Picchu** and **Cusco** can take longer to explore than anticipated. Always leave extra time to appreciate the beauty and history without feeling rushed.

2. Ignoring Altitude Sickness:

- **Altitude sickness** is common in high-altitude areas like Cusco and the Sacred Valley. Acclimate by resting for a couple of days, staying hydrated, and drinking **coca tea** to alleviate symptoms.

3. Failing to Book in Advance:

- **Machu Picchu** and the **Inca Trail** require booking in advance, particularly during high season. **Tickets for Machu Picchu** can sell out months ahead, so it's best to secure your spot early.

4. Not Carrying Enough Cash:

- In rural areas and smaller towns, **cash** is essential, as cards are often not accepted. Always have enough **S/** for local expenses.

5. Skipping Travel Insurance:

- Travel insurance is crucial. It covers medical emergencies, cancellations, and lost luggage, so it's highly recommended to buy a policy before you leave home.

18.4 What to Pack for Peru

Clothing:

- **Layering is essential** due to varying climates across Peru.
  - **High-altitude areas** (Cusco, Sacred Valley): Pack warm clothing even in the dry season (May–October).
  - **Amazon region**: Lightweight, breathable clothes with long sleeves for insect protection.
  - **Coastal cities** (Lima): Light clothes, plus a jacket for cool evenings.

Footwear:

- Comfortable **walking shoes** for city exploration and sturdy **hiking boots** for trekking.

Miscellaneous Items:

- **Sunscreen** and **hat** for sun protection at high altitudes.
- **Insect repellent**: A must for visits to the Amazon.
- **Reusable water bottle**: Staying hydrated is important, especially in high altitudes.
- **Camera & extra memory cards**: Peru's landscapes are picturesque—be ready to capture them!

18.5 Keeping Your Belongings Safe

1. Watch for Pickpockets:

- Cities like **Lima** and **Cusco** can attract pickpockets, especially in crowded areas. Keep your belongings close, use a **money belt**, or secure backpack with zippers.

2. Use Hotel Safes:

- Store passports, cash, and valuables in the **hotel safe** when you're not using them.

3. Be Aware of Scams:

- Common scams include inflated taxi fares, fake tour guides, and street performers asking for money. Always agree on a price beforehand and seek trusted recommendations for tours.

4. Protect Your Electronics:

- Keep electronics secure with **anti-theft backpacks** or locks. Avoid using public Wi-Fi for sensitive transactions—consider using a **VPN**.

5. Invest in Travel Insurance:

- Always travel with **insurance** for coverage on medical expenses, lost luggage, and cancellations.

Chapter 19: Beyond the Guidebook: Hidden Gems of Peru

While Peru is renowned for its iconic destinations like Machu Picchu and the Sacred Valley, the true essence of the country often lies in the hidden corners far from the typical tourist path. This chapter highlights Peru's lesser-known treasures—remote destinations, off-the-beaten-path ruins, and authentic local experiences. These hidden gems offer a deeper connection to Peru's rich history, diverse landscapes, and vibrant culture. Prepare to step off the well-trodden path and discover the magic of Peru's lesser-known wonders.

19.1 Off-the-Beaten-Path Destinations

1. Kuelap - The "Machu Picchu of the North"

- **Location**: Amazonas Region, Northern Peru
- **Why Visit**: Kuelap is a massive stone fortress built by the pre-Incan Chachapoya civilization, predating Machu Picchu by centuries. Perched on a mountaintop, the ruins are far less crowded and just as impressive, with

remarkable stone walls, terracing, and stunning panoramic views of the surrounding cloud forests.

- **Pricing**: Entrance fee: **S/ 20–S/ 30**
- **Getting There**: Kuelap is accessible by a 2-hour drive from the city of **Chachapoyas**. A cable car service has been introduced, making the journey to the site even more scenic.

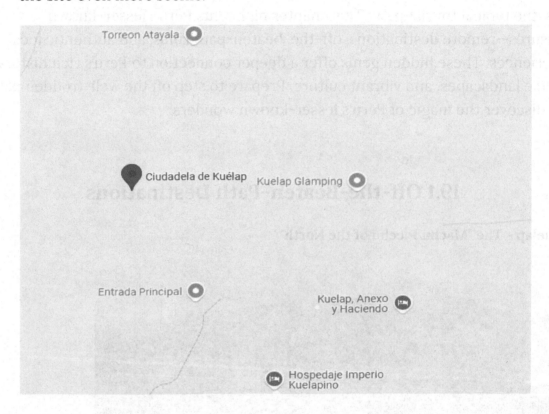

2. The Colca Canyon

- **Location**: Arequipa Region, Southern Peru
- **Why Visit**: Although it's becoming better known, the Colca Canyon remains a hidden gem when compared to the popular destinations of Peru. The canyon is twice as deep as the Grand Canyon and offers a peaceful escape with awe-inspiring views, local villages, and the chance to spot the majestic Andean condor.
- **Pricing**: Entrance fee: **S/ 70–S/ 100**
- **Getting There**: Accessible by bus from **Arequipa** (4–5 hours) or as part of organized tours.
- **Highlights**: **Condor Cross**, **Chivay**, and the thermal springs of **La Calera**.

3. Vilcabamba: The Valley of Longevity

- **Location**: La Convención Province, Cusco Region
- **Why Visit**: Known as the "Valley of Longevity," Vilcabamba offers an incredible mix of history, mystery, and natural beauty. Nestled between the mountains, this valley was once the last refuge of the Inca Empire. The region is perfect for trekking, with its lush landscapes, hidden waterfalls, and ancient Inca terraces.
- **Pricing**: Free entry to the valley; trekking tours can range from **S/ 60–S/ 150**.
- **Getting There**: Vilcabamba is accessible by a 3-hour drive from **Cusco** to the town of **Santa Teresa**, followed by a short trek to the valley.
- **Website**: http://www.vilcabamba-peru.com

19.2 Lesser-Known Inca Ruins

1. Sacsayhuamán

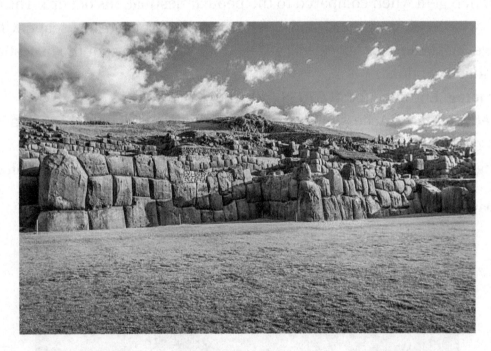

- **Location**: Cusco Region
- **Why Visit**: While **Sacsayhuamán** is often overshadowed by Machu Picchu, it remains a fascinating archaeological site. With its gigantic stones and strategic hilltop location, it's one of the most impressive examples of Inca

stonework. Unlike the crowds at Machu Picchu, you can explore Sacsayhuamán in relative peace, taking in the views of **Cusco**.

- **Pricing**: Entrance fee: **S/ 70** (for the archaeological park)
- **Getting There**: A 20-minute walk from the main square of **Cusco**, or a short taxi ride.
- **Website**: https://www.peru.travel

2. Choquequirao

- **Location**: Cusco Region
- **Why Visit**: Often referred to as the "sister" of Machu Picchu, **Choquequirao** is a hidden Inca city located deep in the Andes. Accessible only by a challenging 4-day trek, Choquequirao is surrounded by stunning scenery and offers a more authentic, less commercialized experience compared to other Inca sites.
- **Pricing**: Entrance fee: **S/ 60**
- **Getting There**: A difficult trek from **Cachora** (5-7 hours), or by guided tour.
- **Highlights**: Terraces, plazas, and Inca structures partially reclaimed by the jungle.

19.3 Remote Villages & Untouched Nature

1. The Community of Ollantaytambo

- **Location**: Sacred Valley, Cusco Region
- **Why Visit**: While **Ollantaytambo** is a well-known town for those heading to Machu Picchu, the nearby rural villages remain far more tranquil. These villages offer visitors a chance to experience authentic **Quechua** culture, with families living much as they have for centuries. You can explore the area on foot or by bike, visiting local farms, weaving cooperatives, and traditional homes.
- **Pricing**: Free to explore the villages; private tours typically cost **S/ 50–S/ 150**.
- **Getting There**: A short distance from **Ollantaytambo** town.
- **Website**: http://www.ollantaytambo.travel

2. The Uros Floating Islands of Lake Titicaca

- **Location**: Lake Titicaca, Puno Region
- **Why Visit**: The **Uros Islands** are one of the world's most unique living environments. Built from totora reeds, these floating islands are home to the **Uros people**, who have lived on the lake for centuries. Visiting the islands gives a rare insight into a vibrant indigenous culture and a chance to explore the stunning scenery of the highest navigable lake in the world.
- **Pricing**: Boat tours from **S/ 50** to **S/ 150**.
- **Getting There**: Boat trips depart from **Puno**, taking about 30 minutes.
- **Website**: https://www.peru.travel

19.4 Local Experiences You Won't Find in Guidebooks

1. Participating in Local Festivals

- **Why Visit**: Peru's festivals are colorful, energetic, and deeply rooted in tradition. From the **Inti Raymi** festival in Cusco, celebrating the Inca sun god, to the **Fiesta de la Virgen de la Candelaria** in Puno, there's always a local celebration happening somewhere. These festivals provide an opportunity to experience Peru's vibrant culture and connect with locals.

- **Pricing**: Varies by event. Many festivals are free, though ticketed events for dances or special performances can range from **S/ 30–S/ 100**.
- **Getting There**: Festivals occur year-round, with the most famous happening between June and August.
- **Website**: https://www.peru.travel

2. Visiting a Traditional Andean Weaving Village

- **Why Visit**: In the towns of **Chinchero** and **Ccaqulle** (near Cusco), you can visit **Andean weaving communities** where women continue ancient textile traditions. Watch the entire process, from dyeing wool with natural plants to weaving intricate patterns. You can also purchase beautiful, hand-woven products directly from the artisans.
- **Pricing**: A typical weaving demonstration costs around **S/ 30–S/ 60**.
- **Getting There**: A short drive from **Cusco** (about 30 minutes).
- **Website**: http://www.peru.travel

Chapter 20: Conclusion

As your journey through Peru draws to a close, you will likely find yourself reflecting on the profound experiences, breathtaking landscapes, and deep cultural connections that have shaped your adventure. Peru is a country of contrasts—where ancient history meets modern vibrancy, and where every region offers a new set of wonders to explore. Whether you've hiked the Inca Trail, marveled at the Nazca Lines, or immersed yourself in the richness of local traditions, Peru has left its mark on you.

This final chapter wraps up your journey with essential tips for a smooth transition back home, as well as advice on how to continue your connection with Peru and its people long after you've returned.

20.1 Wrapping Up Your Peru Journey

As you prepare to leave, it's important to reflect on the diverse and unforgettable experiences you've had. Peru offers more than just stunning landscapes and ancient ruins—it's a place where you can truly connect with the past, present, and future of a remarkable nation. To wrap up your Peru journey:

- **Take Time to Reflect**: Spend your last few days revisiting some of your favorite spots or finding a quiet place to relax and reflect on your experiences. Whether it's a café in Lima, a scenic viewpoint in Cusco, or a quiet corner by Lake Titicaca, Peru's beauty will stay with you long after you leave.
- **Pack Thoughtfully**: Ensure you have everything packed, including souvenirs, gifts, and travel documentation. Take note of any items that are difficult to find back home—Peruvian textiles, jewelry, and unique handicrafts make perfect mementos. Don't forget to check your flight details and make any necessary arrangements for transportation back to the airport.
- **Celebrate Your Achievements**: If you've trekked to Machu Picchu or completed an arduous hike in the Andes, take pride in what you've accomplished. These physical challenges often lead to emotional rewards, and the memories of such experiences will last a lifetime.

20.2 Final Tips & Words of Advice

Before you leave, here are a few final tips and words of advice to ensure your journey ends smoothly and that you have everything in order for your return:

- **Cultural Sensitivity**: Peru is a country rich in indigenous traditions and cultures. Always approach local customs with respect, whether it's during a visit to a village, while observing sacred rituals, or when engaging with locals.
- **Cash and Cards**: While major cities like Lima and Cusco have a variety of ATMs and banks, rural areas may not always have easy access to them. It's advisable to carry some cash (soles) for small purchases, local transport, or tips. Keep your cards and cash in separate locations for security.
- **Health**: After traveling to high-altitude regions like Cusco or the Sacred Valley, it's important to take it easy in your final days. Drink plenty of water, avoid heavy meals, and let your body adjust before embarking on any strenuous activity.
- **Wildlife & Nature**: If you've explored the Amazon or visited wildlife reserves, remember that conservation and respect for the natural environment is key. Be mindful of your impact and avoid disturbing wildlife.
- **Keep in Touch**: It can be tempting to rush home after such an intense adventure, but try to take a moment to express your gratitude. Whether it's sending a thank-you note to a guide, donating to a local charity, or keeping in touch with newfound friends, your connection with Peru doesn't have to end when you board your flight.

20.3 Staying in Touch with Peru: Resources & Communities

Even after you've returned home, staying connected to Peru and its people is a rewarding experience. Here are some ways to keep your Peru connection alive:

- **Online Communities**: Engage with travel forums, blogs, and social media communities to keep up with the latest news from Peru. Websites like **Peru.travel**, **TripAdvisor**, and **Lonely Planet** offer user-generated content and travel tips. Follow local bloggers and influencers who specialize in Peruvian travel, food, and culture for ongoing inspiration.

- **Volunteering & Social Impact**: If you're passionate about making a positive impact, consider participating in **community-based tourism** or **volunteer programs**. Organizations like **Planeterra Foundation** support local communities by providing tourism training and sustainable development. Volunteering opportunities in areas like education, healthcare, and environmental conservation can keep you connected to the country long-term.

- **Cultural Organizations**: Look for cultural exchange programs or organizations that promote Peruvian heritage abroad. Organizations like the **Instituto Cultural Peruano Norteamericano (ICPNA)** in various cities offer events and workshops focused on Peruvian culture and arts.

- **Peruvian Cuisine at Home**: Continue exploring Peruvian flavors at home by learning to cook traditional dishes. Many online resources, like **Peru Delights** or **The Peruvian Kitchen**, offer recipes for dishes like ceviche, lomo saltado, and ají de gallina, allowing you to recreate a piece of Peru in your own kitchen.

- **Return Visits**: Peru is a country that offers something new each time you visit. Many travelers return to explore new regions, discover lesser-known treasures, or reconnect with people they met during their first visit. Consider planning another trip, perhaps during a different season, to experience a different side of Peru.

Final Thoughts

Peru is a land of mystery and wonder—its history, culture, and landscapes create an experience unlike any other. From the timeless ruins of the Incas to the vibrant streets of Lima, every corner of the country offers a story to tell and a journey to be had. By planning thoughtfully, staying respectful of local traditions, and remaining open to new experiences, you can create a lifelong connection to this incredible destination.

Whether you're reliving memories of your journey or planning to return, Peru will continue to inspire and enrich your life long after you've left its shores. Safe travels, and may the spirit of the Andes guide you on your next adventure!

Made in the USA
Coppell, TX
09 December 2024

42039925R00072